Computerized Library Catalogs: Their Growth, Cost and Utility, by J. L. Dolby, V. J. Forsyth, H. L. Resnikoff. Cambridge, Mass.: M.I.T. Press. 164 pp. $10.

This study made under an Office of Education grant says automate all but the smallest library catalog. The report is a feasibility study using data from a medium-sized university library. The authors are all affiliated with the R&D Consultants Company, Los Altos, California. Of use to all librarians because it offers a method of cost analysis on cataloging and its automation—frantically needed in the profession. *Jan. 1970*

American libraries 1: 89

Computerized Library Catalogs:
Their Growth, Cost, and Utility

COMPUTERIZED LIBRARY CATALOGS: THEIR GROWTH, COST, AND UTILITY

J. L. DOLBY
V. J. FORSYTH
H. L. RESNIKOFF

THE M.I.T. PRESS
Cambridge, Massachusetts, and London, England

The research reported herein was performed pursuant to a contract with the Office of Education, U.S. Department of Health, Education, and Welfare. Contractors undertaking such projects under Government sponsorship are encouraged to express freely their professional judgment in the conduct of the project. Points of view or opinions stated do not, therefore, necessarily represent official Office of Education position or policy.

SBN 262 04023 9 (hardcover)
Library of Congress catalog card number: 70-84655

Table of Contents

Preface

This book is a slightly modified form of a report on computerized library catalogs prepared for the Office of Education of the United States Department of Health, Education, and Welfare (Contract OEC-1-7-071182-5013). It consists of seven chapters. The first poses the problems that have been studied, introduces background material to facilitate an understanding of their significance, and presents our conclusions and general recommendations. The remaining chapters belong to one of two parts, depending on whether their principle concern is the *utility* or the *cost* of computerized library catalogs. Because the problem of utility is the more speculative of the two, it has been placed in the second part.

For the most part, our methods have been analytical and statistical. Wherever possible, every attempt has been made to examine the dynamic aspects of the problem under consideration because they offer deeper insights into the fundamental processes affecting libraries than static, local, or parochial analyses possibly can. One consequence of this methodological principle has been a concentration of effort on the collection and analysis of statistical time series related to the growth, use, and structure of libraries. The results are inextricably intertwined with the problem of utility and the means for resolving it.

A detailed examination of several large university and public libraries shows that mature libraries grow at a rate very close to the rate of growth of the Gross National Product, and personnel costs tend to grow at a somewhat faster rate. As the size of the collection increases, the amount of access-per-item must also increase if adequate user access is to be insured. On the other hand, the cost of computation is decreasing rapidly, and the technology to make use of computers in processing bibliographic records is at hand. Therefore, the primary conclusion emerging from this study is that mechanization of the cataloging function is not only desirable and necessary, but also inevitable.

A tutorial note may be in order for some readers. Throughout this book we use various kinds of graph paper—not all of it "regular" graph paper

vii

with linear scales in each direction. The value of graphic representation is seldom questioned. The utility of the particular types of graph papers used here is well known to workers in mathematics and the physical sciences though not so well known in the social sciences and humanities. The value in using nonlinear scales in graphs usually is that the distortion of the scale distorts curves into straight lines. This simplifies the problem of "fitting" a curve to the data, as it is generally easier to choose a straight line, with the aid of a transparent straightedge, than it is to choose a curve. It is also more obvious how a straight line is to be extended in either direction than it is for a curve.

One of the essential points of this report is the concern with growth in libraries and the impact this has on library operations. Libraries tend to grow at a fixed percentage growth each year rather than a fixed absolute growth. If one plots the holdings of a library against time on "regular" graph paper (with both the horizontal and vertical scales divided into equal increments) one obtains a curve that is known in mathematics as the *exponential curve.* If the vertical scale is properly compressed, this curve is literally straightened out into a straight line.

The proper scale compression is provided by replacing the equally divided (or "linear") scale with a logarithmic scale. Fortunately, graph paper manufacturing concerns have long stocked a variety of papers with different logarithmic scales. Such paper is called semilogarithmic paper and is widely used in what follows (see, for example, Figure 1).

The other two types of graph paper used in this report are more specialized. The first is logarithmic graph paper where both scales are logarithmic (hence this is sometimes called "log-log" paper) (see Figure 8). This paper has a wide variety of uses, but its use in this report occurs primarily because of the need to portray situations where both scales of the plot exhibit considerable changes in value. On a logarithmic scale, the distance between one and ten is the same as the distance between ten and a hundred, or between ten thousand and a hundred thousand. Hence, log-log paper is a natural candidate when the two variables that determine the plotted point are each subject to order-of-magnitude changes in the given data.

Finally, we have also made use of "normal probability paper." This paper is so scaled that the cumulative rendering of the frequencies of a normal distribution will plot as a straight line. This paper is widely used as a quick check on the approximate normality of a set of observations and is so used here (Fig. 14).

The authors wish to express their appreciation to the many people who gave freely of their time and knowledge so that we could accumulate the information on which this study is based. We are especially grateful to H.

D. Avram (Library of Congress), The Honorable George Bush (Representative in Congress from Texas), R. De Gennaro (Harvard University), R. C. Goodwell (Los Angeles County Public Library), R. D. Johnson (Stanford University), B. Markuson (Library of Congress), G. B. Moreland (Montgomery County, Maryland, Department of Public Libraries), R. O'Keeffe (Rice University), F. Palmer (Harvard University), D. Remington (Bro-Dart Industries), R. Shoffner (Institute for Library Research, Berkeley), and A. Veaner (Stanford University) for their important contributions of catalogs, samples, cost figures, and other technical data critical for the success of this work.

We are also greatly indebted to Mr. Eugene Kennedy and Mr. F. Kurt Cylke of the Office of Education for their full support throughout the course of this study and for valuable comments on the completed report. Mr. Maurice Line (Bath Institute of Technology) and Mr. Eugene Graziano (University of California at Santa Barbara) also read the report in full and presented valuable insight into some of the problems we consider.

It is customary for authors to acknowledge the encouragement and sacrifice of their families, and with good reason. Continuing this excellent tradition, we dedicate this book to our families.

J. L. Dolby
V. J. Forsyth
H. L. Resnikoff

Los Altos, California
January 1969

1 Introduction: Computerized Library Catalogs: Their Growth, Cost, and Utility

1.1 Computerization of Library Catalogs

To "computerize" or "automate" a library catalog means to put it into machine-readable form. The catalogs of interest in this regard are usually one or more of the shelf, author, title, and subject lists, most of which are now generally maintained as card catalogs. It is presumed that computerized catalogs will reduce the unit cost of reference, permit the production of book catalogs and special-purpose bibliographies, and provide library management with regular, detailed, and timely summaries of major aspects of the library's activities. These advantages must be balanced against the costs of conversion of the retrospective file to machine-readable form, operation of the computerized catalog system, and updating the catalog.

Conversion of the retrospective file must be done only once. The cost of doing this—which depends upon the state of technology when the conversion is attempted and what parts of the file records are chosen for computerization, as well as on the size of the file—can be accurately estimated from accessible and reliable data. Because the technology of converting printed materials to machine-readable form is changing rapidly, these estimates must be current. Similarly, the cost of operating a computerized catalog system can be accurately calculated if the type of equipment to be used is known and if the computer programs that implement the operations are available. The third cost area, concerned with updating the computerized catalog, involves variables about which little is known but which dominate the economic analysis. These include the rate of growth of the collection, the rate of growth of funds allocated to the library, their relationship to circulation and other forms of use.

1.2. Library Growth Rates

The natural measure of library size is the number of items held in the collection. Annual growth is the difference in size for consecutive years.

Most size estimates are open to question because there is no uniform method of counting holdings; some libraries count pamphlets and individual issues or volumes of serials acquired, whereas others provide what is equivalent to a count of the number of cards present in the shelf list. In many cases size estimates spanning several decades are not publicly available.

Gross estimates for the Library of Congress, which can be obtained from the World Almanacs, show that its size increases exponentially with time, if relatively minor fluctuations of short duration are excepted. For the interval 1924-66, the average growth for the Library of Congress was between 3 and 4 percent per year so that the number of holdings doubled every 18 to 24 years. Although the Library of Congress is unique in many ways, its pattern of growth is the natural and common one.

Instead of measuring the growth of a library by counting the total number of items held each year, one can use another method which enjoys two important advantages: it permits a precise definition of what is counted, and it can be applied to the collections of libraries that have not kept growth statistics. This method involves the number of items held in the collection arranged by date of imprint, information which can be obtained from samples of the shelf or title list. Those items that do not have an imprint date are not counted. Serial publications are not counted either because neither the shelf nor title list normally provides imprint data for them. This measure is closely related to the traditional ways of describing library growth and size.

The Library of Congress is established, large, and publicly supported; Stanford University's Undergraduate Library was founded in 1966 and consisted then of 25,000 titles. Figure 1 shows the distribution of titles by decade of imprint from a one-tenth uniform sample drawn from the 1966 Subject Catalog for the Stanford Undergraduate Library.[1] Growth by decade is exponential apart from minor irregularities, which are most notable during the decades of The Great War and the Second World War. The doubling period is about ten years, which corresponds to annual growth rate of approximately 7 percent. The collection contains fewer titles imprinted prior to 1880 than the exponential distribution requires; this is probably a consequence of its undergraduate orientation.

The shelf list of the Widener Library at Harvard University is being converted to machine-readable form, and subject-related subsets of it have

---

[1]Figure 1 and many of the other text figures are drawn on *semi-logarithmic* graph paper. On such paper the vertical scale distances measure the logarithms of the data values, so that exponential growth will correspond to a straight line.

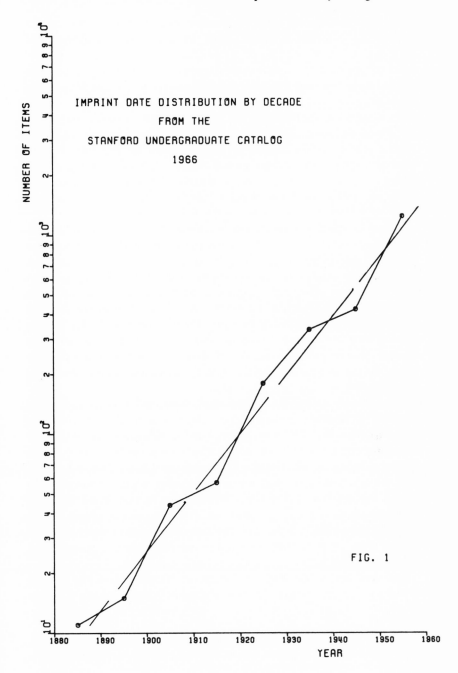

IMPRINT DATE DISTRIBUTION BY DECADE
FROM THE
STANFORD UNDERGRADUATE CATALOG
1966

FIG. 1

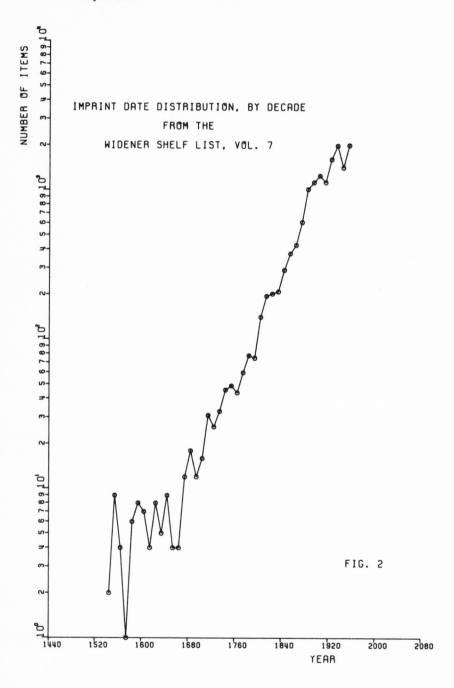

IMPRINT DATE DISTRIBUTION, BY DECADE
FROM THE
WIDENER SHELF LIST, VOL. 7

FIG. 2

been published. Volume 7, Bibliography and Bibliography Periodicals, published in 1966, lists more than 18,000 titles, whose imprint date distribution is displayed in Figure 2 from 1540-49 through 1950-59 by decade. With the exception of the earliest years—through 1669—and the usual fluctuations, the trend is exponential again. The number of titles by imprint decade doubles in about 35 years during this 300-year interval, equivalent to 2 percent annual growth.

History can be read from Figure 2. Valleys in the imprint distribution mean relatively small acquisitions, which often correspond to periods of unstable social and economic conditions. The relative minimum at the decade whose mid-year was 1945 exhibits the effect of World War II; the previous relative minimum, the Great War. Although the number of items grew during the decade of the American Civil War, the growth rate declined as the graph shows, and there was almost no growth at all from the 1820's to the 1830's, a period of revolution and financial panics. The French Revolution highlighted the decade of the 1790's, which displays another relative minimum in the figure, and so on.

Annual variations in the imprint distribution magnify the effects of external influences; these are shown in Figure 3 for the 1830-1965 period. The world wars and the Great Depression (which had a worldwide effect) stand out as the major social phenomena of the era. In addition to providing qualitative indications of major historical events, a measure of historical significance can be constructed using the statistical data that underlies Figures 2 and 3.

A random sample drawn from the shelf list of the Fondren Library at Rice University also has an exponential imprint date distribution (cp. Figure 18). Thus imprint distributions from three quite different university libraries and the Library of Congress size distribution all grow exponentially apart from local fluctuations. Their doubling period and annual growth rates are gathered in Table 1. Additional data for university libraries is given in Figure 4 for 1965-6.[2]

These exponential library growth rates are instances of the much bruited "information explosion"; they exhibit the explosion and provide a measure of it. But the data make it clear that there has always been a

---

[2]Figure 4 and some other text figures are drawn on logarithmic graph paper, where distances along both scales measure the logarithms of quantities. On such paper a straight line corresponds to a function of the form $y = ax^b$. Lines parallel to the diagonal drawn from the lower left hand corner to the upper right hand corner represent quantities that are proportional. This is the case in Figure 4, where the advantage in using logarithmic paper is the compression of the picture to a reasonable size.

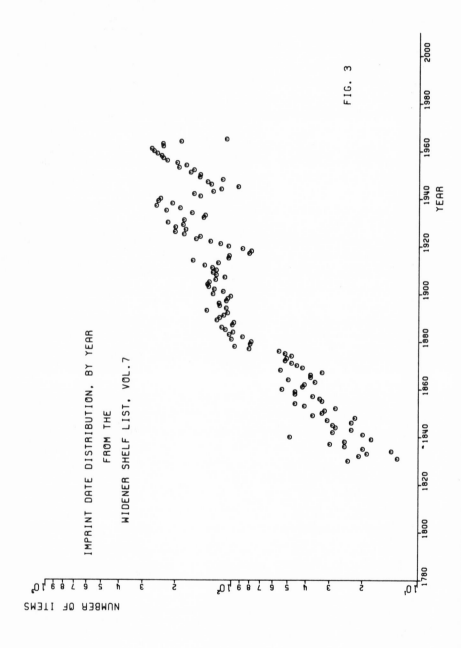

IMPRINT DATE DISTRIBUTION, BY YEAR
FROM THE
WIDENER SHELF LIST, VOL.7

FIG. 3

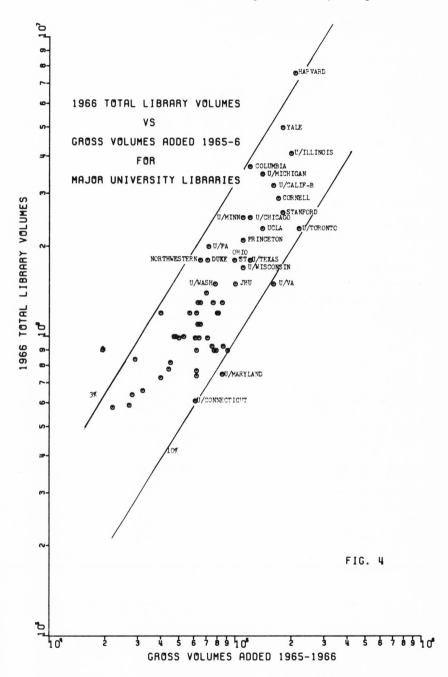

FIG. 4

Source: "Resources of Texas Libraries" (E. G. Holley and D. D. Hendricks), Texas State Library, Austin, Texas, 1968.

Table 1 Library Doubling Periods and Annual Long-Term Growth Rates

	Doubling Period, years	Growth Rate, percent
Library of Congress	18 to 24	3 to 4
Stanford University		
Undergraduate	10	7
Widener (Vol. 7)	32 to 35	2 to 2.3
Fondren	21 to 24	3 to 3.5

library explosion—at least for the past several hundred years—and in the past it has always been possible to cope with rapid growth. It will be possible to continue to cope with such growth in the future if, but only if, the rate of growth is not greater than the rate of expansion of the national economy. This and related questions are studied in Chapter 6. The conclusion is that most libraries grow more rapidly than population but more slowly than the Gross National Product economic indicator. Consequently, the economy should be able to maintain and assimilate the "explosive" growth of library holdings.

The significance of exponential growth for computerization of catalogs is that the task of updating the computerized file is potentially the most difficult and costly. If an average doubling period of 20 years is assumed (it has actually been less for most university collections in recent decades) and if a retrospective file has been computerized, then the next 20 years will provide about the same number of additional titles that must be merged into the computerized system, and in the following twenty years twice as many will have to be assimilated. For a library with a two-million item retrospective file, the updating costs at the end of forty years will be running at an annual rate more than half of that initially required to convert the retrospective file to computerized form. This estimate does not account for technological advances or monetary inflation. After 60 years the annual updating costs will have outpaced the initial annual computerization costs. For faster growing libraries these time intervals will be shorter. Special attention should be paid to the updating problem and in particular to means that will enable libraries to jointly solve it.

1.3. Acquisitions Expenditures and Related Quantities

In the previous section it was stated that acquisitions growth is exponential but limited by total economic growth. Acquisitions growth is also related to total library expenditures, and in the case of public libraries it is related both to the size of the population taxed to support the library and to circulation.

Figure 5 exhibits acquisitions expenditures as a function of the population taxed for support for the largest public library in each state. States that are not represented did not provide us with the necessary data. Although the data points are scattered throughout the diagram, a general trend curve, which is a line on the log graph paper used for the illustration, runs from Vermont and Wyoming up through New York and Illinois. The slope of the line is almost exactly 1, which means that acquisitions expenditures are effectively proportional to taxed population, if the considerable scatter in the diagram is ignored. The states with the lowest ratios of expenditures to taxed population are (in increasing order) South Carolina, Louisiana, New Mexico, and Alabama. Those with the highest ratios are (in decreasing order) Maine, Florida, Indiana, and Virginia.

Because an increase in taxed population does not always correspond to increased taxes collected, the data used for Figure 5 is not as highly correlated as would be statistics based on personal income or gross state product (in analogy with gross national product). Figure 6 shows what happens when state personal income is used; income data for 1957–a decade earlier than the acquisitions data, to allow time for income growth to influence budgeted expenditures (cp. Chapter 6 for a discussion of this point)–shows that acquisition expenditures are proportional to state personal income (i.e., the slope of the trend line is 1). The states with small acquisitions-to-income ratios are South Carolina, Connecticut, New Jersey, Arkansas, North Carolina, and Alabama, in that order. Although there are certain biases inherent in Figure 6 which complicate interpretation, such as the varying proportion of state population represented by the city or county taxed to support the (largest public) library represented by the data, it is still reasonable to conclude that the states just named are those that are not doing their share in maintaining their major public library collection. In the passage from Figure 5 to Figure 6, Louisiana has moved from below average to average in its acquisitions expenditures. This simply means that this state is doing what it can in terms of available income. Connecticut and New Jersey are both laggards. They are also bedroom states, sending a large portion of their working populations to New York City and Philadelphia, and undoubtedly making use of the major library facilities provided by these cities (the New York State and Pennsylvania entries in Figures 5 and 6 are for the libraries of these cities). This is an illustration of the financial burden that is borne by the major cities to provide services that are used by the suburban population. The high ratio states are, in decreasing order, Tennessee, Colorado, Oregon, Hawaii, and Illinois.

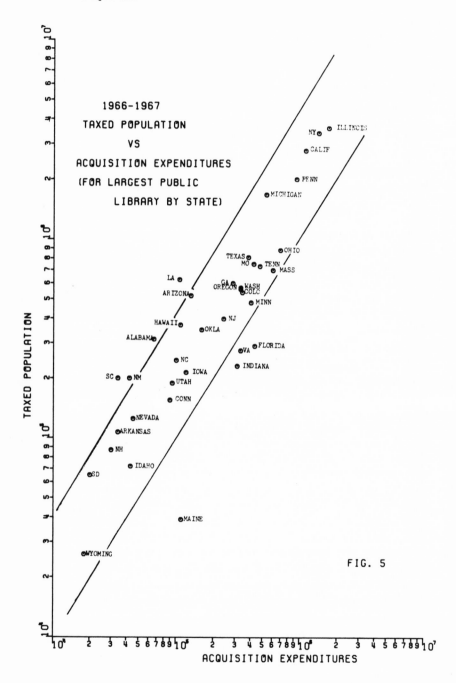

FIG. 5

Source: Statistical summaries supplied by various state libraries.

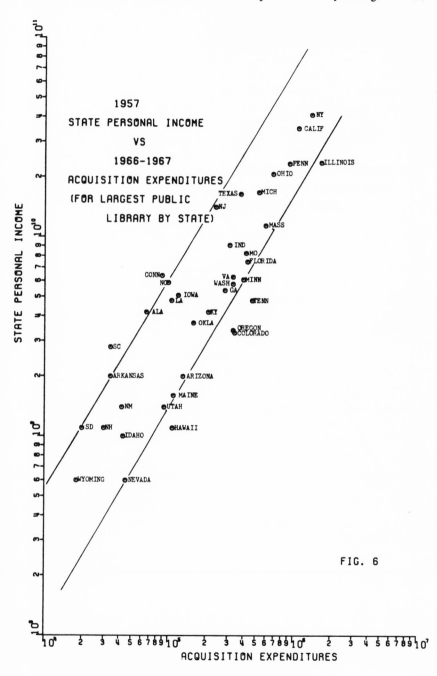

STATE PERSONAL INCOME

1957

STATE PERSONAL INCOME

VS

1966-1967

ACQUISITION EXPENDITURES

(FOR LARGEST PUBLIC

LIBRARY BY STATE)

FIG. 6

ACQUISITION EXPENDITURES

Sources: "U.S. Income & Output," U.S. Dept. of Commerce, 1958, pp. 156-157 and
Statistical summaries supplied by various state libraries.

The number of items acquired is approximately proportional to expenditures. We have already established that library growth rates are exponential; moreover, the previous illustrations show that expenditures for acquisitions are approximately proportional to Gross Personal Income, which in turn is proportional to Gross National Product. It has long been known that Gross National Product grows exponentially, subject to local fluctuations, so these relations are mutually consistent (cp. Chapter 6).

Another conclusion of exceptional significance can be drawn from the fact that most libraries lie close to the trend line in Figure 6, no matter what their size. Since libraries grow exponentially with time, it follows that they will move up along the trend line in Figure 6 at an exponential rate; thus it is possible to predict the future properties of small or medium sized libraries by examination of those that are now large. We have taken pains to show the essential proportionality of acquisitions expenditures and quantities like taxed population, personal income, and in what follows, circulation, in order to obtain this important result.

Figure 7, Circulation vs. Total Book Stock, confirms the proportionality of library size and circulation for the largest public library in each state for which data is available. There are approximately three circulations per book of stock.

1.4. Public and University Libraries

Public and university libraries differ in many ways, but the larger ones of each kind tend to be more similar than the smaller. This is due to the increasing dominance of the archival component of the library as it grows. The archival component is that part used almost solely for research purposes and which has a low circulation rate. As it is the large libraries that are currently most concerned with computerization, and stand to profit most from it, this study will apply to both public and university libraries.

Figure 8 shows that universities generally spend a greater portion of each visible budget dollar on acquisitions than do public libraries but that the larger public libraries approach the university rate.

This brief analysis, although superficial in nature, is sufficient to show that historical library growth rates closely parallel growth in the Gross National Product and that the relative acquisition rates of public libraries in the various states closely parallel the relative size of personal incomes in the states. These two observations suggest that library growth is determined by the growth in the economy. If this is true, the capability of the public and university library systems to cope with the so-called "information explosion" in the future depends first on a continued growth in the

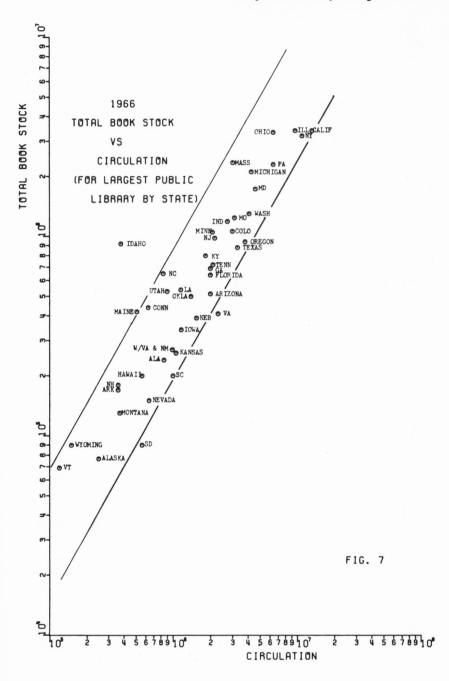

FIG. 7

Source: Statistical summaries supplied by various state libraries.

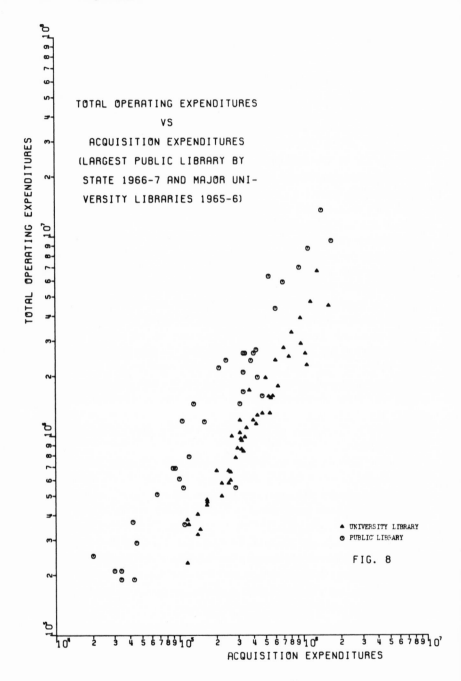

TOTAL OPERATING EXPENDITURES
VS
ACQUISITION EXPENDITURES
(LARGEST PUBLIC LIBRARY BY
STATE 1966-7 AND MAJOR UNI-
VERSITY LIBRARIES 1965-6)

▲ UNIVERSITY LIBRARY
◎ PUBLIC LIBRARY

FIG. 8

TOTAL OPERATING EXPENDITURES

ACQUISITION EXPENDITURES

Sources: Statistical summaries supplied by various state libraries and "Library Statistics of Colleges & Universities, 1965-1966," 1967, ALA.

economic strength in the country and second on the ability of librarians to maintain their cost per book circulated (or stored) on a reasonably constant level.

A study by D. S. Culbertson (Ref. 1) suggests that over the past 80 years libraries have been fighting a losing battle with costs: according to his information, libraries spent about three-fourths of their budget for acquisitions in the 1880's and one-fourth of their budget for personnel costs, but that by the 1960's this ratio had been inverted. This increase can be accounted for by the facts that salaries have consistently increased and that larger libraries generally must spend a greater proportion of their time locating specific items.

Thus libraries are faced with a three-front battle in managing their overall costs: the exponential growth of the materials they must acquire, the exponential growth of the salaries of their personnel, and a growing need to provide more access-per-item to their collections due to their increased size. Little can be done about the exponential growth of available materials despite the occasional suggestion that publication should be restricted by legislation or fiat. Indeed, although we have postulated that economic growth is the essential restriction on library growth, it may well be that economic growth is a direct correlate of our ability to make available appropriate information. It is possible to argue that librarians can make better use of their personnel through careful time and motion studies and proper planning based on such studies (see, for example, Reference 2). Such improvements are, unfortunately, one-time improvements. They may buy a given library enough increased productivity to offset growth for a year, or two, or even ten, but they cannot solve the essential problem.

The only method that society has found for increasing productivity exponentially is by increasing use of mechanization. In the library, the central tasks revolve about the construction and use of the catalog. Until the catalog has been mechanized, a library cannot be said to be "automated" to a reasonable degree. Catalog automation not only provides the opportunity to increase productivity in a crucial area of library activity, but it also provides an economically feasible way to extend access-per-item to library holdings through publication of printed catalogs, through special bibliographies, and through direct on-line interrogation of the catalog by computer.

1.5. Conclusions

Over the long term, mature libraries grow at a rate very close to the rate of growth of the Gross National Product when measured in constant dollars. Personnel costs tend to grow at a somewhat faster rate. Librarians can only cope with exponential expansion if they are able to obtain an ever-increasing proportion of the resources of the economy or if they are able to expand the productivity of their personnel at a rate sufficient to offset the increases in personnel costs.

The technology for mechanizing important library functions is at hand and in use at a number of libraries today. Since construction and maintenance of the catalog is the essential activity of the library, library mechanization implies catalog mechanization. The cost of mechanization is decreasing rapidly, with order of magnitude cost reductions appearing in some areas and with a falling cost of computation that is currently doubling the productivity per dollar every nine months.

From the view point of the user, the continued buildup of library materials posed a substantial problem with manual methods. The larger the file, the greater the need for access-per-item to its contents. Present cataloging practice provides sufficient information to support literally hundreds of different orderings of the catalog and subsets of the catalog. In manual operations, the cost of expanding access beyond present levels goes up at least linearly with the number of access files created. Library budgets already strained by the exponential growth of the cost of personnel and of acquisition cannot absorb the added cost of extra access with manual methods. Mechanization provides the opportunity to generate added access files at very low cost and hence to satisfy the real need of the user in expanding library systems.

In this context, *the primary conclusion of this study is that mechanization of the cataloging function is not only necessary and desirable, but also inevitable.*

The primary deterrent to catalog mechanization is the substantial cost of converting the retrospective file to machine-readable form. With exponential growth this problem will become more formidable as time goes on. In public library systems this cost can be readily absorbed in normal operating budgets because conversion costs will normally be a relatively small proportion of the annual budget and the need for catalogs for a number of branches fits naturally into the mechanization context (see, for example, Reference 8, Chapter 2). In archival libraries conversion costs will be a substantial proportion of a single year's budget and it will be necessary to obtain external funding and/or stretch out the conversion project over several years. Proper strategies exist to allow this to be done in a manner that produces useful (and perhaps saleable) items throughout the course of the conversion process.

Typical conversion of bibliographic records costs approximately 1/5 cent per character, but there is a suggestion that the cost per character is slightly higher in records averaging 400 to 500 characters per record than in records averaging 200 to 300 characters per record.

Conversion costs will vary substantially according to the demands for quality made by the librarian and/or his users. Automatic procedures can be constructed to detect approximately 60 percent of the errors occurring in library records, but use of such procedures will not decrease the over-all cost and may tend to actually increase it due to the larger number of errors caught by the machine that have to be corrected.

Implementation of mechanization will require the availability of modern computing equipment and electronic typesetting devices. Most libraries already have access to the former, and expansion in the latter field is progressing at a sufficiently rapid rate to assure general availability within the next 2 to 4 years.

Implementation will also require an increasing awareness on the part of librarians of the uses of computers and of the intricacies of computer programs. Assembly code programming of library problems is costly, time-consuming, and unnecessary if recourse is had to good macro-oriented languages with proper facilities for linguistic data handling. Such languages exist but are not yet widely used in this field.

At present, the various forms of inputting material to machine-readable form are highly competitive (except for on-line conversion), and the choice of form will be made on other grounds. Output machines are in a process of drastic change with electronic composition machines capable of higher speeds, better quality, and lower cost than line printers now on the market.

Studies of information from the Library of Congress show that the non-English proportion of archival collections is steadily growing, thus broadening the need for larger type fonts and multi-language manipulation procedures to supplement the human activities now necessary to the handling of non-English materials.

Library catalogs contain a wealth of information about the historic development of the many fields of human endeavor and the interrelations that bind these activities. Mechanization of the catalog permits exploitation of this information by workers in many fields of research. Analysis of the same information can greatly assist librarians in studying their own collections and in managing the acquisition of materials for the library. Many studies of this type can be conducted on random samples of the catalog, though more detailed work requires access to the entire collection in machine-readable form.

A means has been provided (in Chapter 7) to determine in advance the number of bibliographic listings that might reasonably be generated from a record of a given structure. This information, together with information about the average number files maintained by libraries of a given size, will help resolve the problem of deciding what is to be included on the machine-readable form of the catalog record.

1.6. Recommendations

1. Over the next decade all but the smallest libraries should plan to automate their cataloging operation as a central part of their plans for over-all automation.

2. The problem of giving a meaningful definition of the "size" of a library should be studied. The size should be stated in terms of one or more numbers that can be readily determined from accessible data for a given library.

3. Libraries should provide more access to library materials by increasing the number of access points to their bibliographic holdings and by increasing the availability of this information to the user community.

4. Both public and university libraries should give greater thought to the possibility of selling printed copies of their catalogs and the special-purpose bibliographies produced from them. Plans for such publication should be based on surveys of public acceptance and on the solicitation of information as to what users want in this direction.

5. Librarians should regularly collect statistics of their holdings from their machine-readable catalog and from new acquisitions information to assist in proper management of their collections.

6. Major archival libraries should regularly publish randomly ordered catalogs of their holdings to simplify the task of obtaining random samples for research purposes and for the guidance of other librarians in their selection of materials.

7. Proper quality control procedures should be set forth at the beginning of any major conversion project; the quality level required and the cost of obtaining that quality should be explicitly set out in any cost study of catalog preparation and maintenance.

8. Prior to beginning conversion of a retrospective catalog, calculations should be made to assure that sufficient information is included in the bibliographic record to support the number of access points (especially bibliographic files) needed for the collection over the next several decades.

9. Librarians should support the development of macro-oriented text-processing languages to reduce programming and operating costs in their operations. Such support should include the specification of speed and ease of use necessary for their applications.

10. In view of the rapid rate of change of computing capabilities, the library community should establish a standing committee to continually monitor the cost of various library computer operations so that individual libraries will have up-to-date information for their costing activities and the computer industry will be informed as to the effect of new developments in technology on their library customers.

11. Librarians should investigate the use of electronic composition devices in composing library catalogs for printing.

12. Library catalogs printed for public use should be printed in 5-6 point condensed type with format chosen to obtain maximum character density per page, consistent with legibility.

13. An in-depth study of library characteristics and their relations with established economic indicators should be made to provide norms and predictors for future library planning.

References

1. Culbertson, Don S., "The Costs of Data Processing in University: in Book Acquisition & Cataloging," *College Research Libraries* 24 (November 1963) 487-489.
2. Kozumplik, William A., "Time and Motion Study of Library Operations," *Special Libraries* (October 1967) 585-588.

PART I: COST

2 An Analysis of Cost Factors in the Automation of Library Catalogs

2.1. Introduction

An analysis of the available literature on the cost of library automation, and in particular on the cost of catalog information, discloses a curious paradox: many papers start out by decrying the lack of reliable information, yet one has no difficulty in locating 50 or more technical papers that discuss various aspects of this complex problem. Further, we find that both librarians and equipment manufacturers are unusually willing to present any information they have that bears on the problem.

The source of this paradox is not hard to find. The cataloging operation in a library is a complex one consisting of a number of definite steps with a number of alternatives for each step. Evaluation of the alternatives depends crucially on the particular library context in which the operations are to be carried out. As a result most of the available information is almost totally concerned with detailed enumeration of these operations and with evaluation of the particular alternatives available to the authors at the time the study was carried out. However, this is not a problem of failing to see the forest for the trees; there are several excellent papers that view the over-all problem from what might be called the "systems" point of view (for examples see References 1, 2, and 3). The problem is rather one of explicitly identifying cost factors according to the relative order of importance in the over-all scheme of things. In simplest terms, one does not start worrying about 10 percent cost variations until order of magnitude cost variations have been settled.

Today there is a plethora of information available on the 10 percent level, and a diligent librarian should have no difficulty in finding sufficient information to enable him to resolve the various decisions that must be made in the context of his own library cost structure. The order of magnitude decisions are harder; they involve factors over which the librarian has only partial control. Yet a realistic evaluation of the problem demands that we enumerate the cost factors in their order of importance.

23

2.2. The Cost to the User

Without question the greatest single cost connected with the library catalog operation is the cost to the user. To evaluate this quantitatively, let us set aside the question of the utility of browsing through the stacks. Some libraries maintain open stacks and others do not. In a small public library it seems reasonable to argue that "pick-up through browsing" accounts for a substantial proportion of the actual circulation. In a large archival library browsing serves a purpose but certainly does not account for anywhere near as large a proportion of the circulation.

Consider a university library with one million items in its collection. Roughly, we can expect that circulation will also be at the one million level and that the annual operating budget will also be in the order of one million dollars. Suppose further that the cataloging operation takes up 10 percent of the total operating budget, or $100,000. Finally, let us suppose that the average user makes use of the catalog once for each time he takes an item out of the stock.

In this context, if it costs the user only ten cents each time he uses the catalog, the collective user cost of the catalog will equal the library's cost of preparing and maintaining it. Or, to put it another way, any change in library procedures that reduces the average cost of catalog use to the user by ten cents will result in an over-all system saving equal to the entire cost of cataloging. One does not have to assign a very high value to the user's time to see that a saving of a minute or two per usage has considerable value from the over-all point of view.

Unfortunately, the cost to the user does not appear in a typical library operating budget, although it is pertinent that some studies have shown that as much as 75 percent of the catalog use is by members of the library staff. However, libraries do operate in an atmosphere where user opinion can be heard. University libraries normally discuss such matters with a faculty library committee.

Public libraries operate in a wide variety of contexts with varying degrees of contact with the general public, business and industry, and other governmental bodies. In almost any context, however, if the librarian can demonstrate that he can provide an order of magnitude improvement in service for a relatively small increase in a minor portion of his operating budget, he will find himself in a strong position.

In this context several authors have noted the need for careful studies of user habits and needs in connection with library activities. We would certainly not oppose the utility of such studies. However, the notion of a "careful" study implies the need for precise estimation, and the real need for this will come only when we have exhausted the order of magnitude gains and are seeking for the remaining marginal improvements.

In particular, we claim that no careful study is necessary to show that a printed catalog on the desk of the user, or at least in the immediate vicinity of his office, is a sufficient advance over the present card catalog to provide a substantial time advantage in his use of the catalog. At the very least, the user is saved a trip to the library for all those searches that prove to be fruitless. Further, in an automated catalog it is feasible to produce many more different orderings of the catalog (and subsets thereof) than is feasible in a card system. This in turn increases the number of access points to the library collection and the over-all utility of the catalog to the user. It may be difficult to put a precise dollar figure on the value of added access, but at the first level it is certainly sufficient to offset minor cost increments in the cataloging operation.

2.3. The Cost of Programming

User cost is necessarily difficult to pin down because it does not appear as a line item in the budget. There is nothing ephemeral about the cost of programming. As De Genarro points out (Ref. 2): "Experience has shown that software costs are as high as hardware costs or even higher." The reason for this is not hard to find. The library has become the first major computer user interested primarily in processing linguistic information (as opposed to numerical information). As such, librarians are forced to pay a high price to operate in a context that was designed for processing financial transactions and/or scientific computations. The two most widely used programming languages are COBOL and FORTRAN. COBOL was designed for the financial community, FORTRAN for the scientific community. No comparable language presently exists for the library community. In an appendix to this chapter we provide a concise technical description of a number of languages that have application to linguistic processing. Here we restrict ourselves to a few comments on the main factors that should be considered in examining any given language for its applicability to a given library problem.

Perhaps the most important feature of a programming language is its "level." Level can be measured by the complexity of the task that can be accomplished in a single instruction. "Higher-level" languages are designed to permit the execution of very complex jobs in a given area with relatively few instructions. From the cost point of view, this means that less programming time is required to accomplish a given task. More importantly, as a computer program must be precisely written if it is to work properly, a higher level language simplifies the task of digging out the program errors and correcting them. Finally, the higher-level language is basically easier to learn as, by definition, the instructions in the higher-level language are closer to representing meaningful units of the task that has to be performed.

To put this in perspective, all machines will have available certain "lower-level" languages usually called "assembly languages" or "user codes." The higher-level language will typically accomplish with one instruction what a lower-level language could do in ten instructions. A professional programmer working with an assembly language will frequently require three months to accomplish a meaningful task. On the other hand, a competent amateur programmer (e.g., a librarian who has learned a higher-level language for application to his problems) might well finish the same task in a week to ten days. In addition to the obvious cost savings in man hours, the use of the higher-level language permits the person with the problem to work out his own solution without the need for the (generally difficult) communication with a specialist in another field. (Where this can be accomplished, the librarian also avoids the need for getting in line for the professional programmer's services, a process that can result in considerable time losses as there is a shortage of professional programmers.)

With all these advantages on the side of higher-level languages, it is only reasonable to ask why anyone would consider assembly languages. The answer lies in the problem of obtaining high speed in operation. The achievement of higher-level languages is accomplished at some cost in the operating speed of the machine. In extreme cases the ratio of speeds is as much as fifty to one; ten-to-one speed differences are not uncommon and two- or three-to-one is what is generally to be expected. For small jobs, these speed losses are offset by the gains in programming costs. For large jobs where the necessary computation is relatively trivial, the time to read the data into the machine and read it out again may be larger than the time to do the necessary internal processing, even with an inefficient higher-level language.

For these purposes, almost any catalog operation must be classed as a large job. Many simple editing tasks will be sufficiently small so as to allow use of higher-level languages without noticeable losses in machine time. However, the more sophisticated use of catalogs on computers, particularly those that will provide substantial increases in access to the information contained in the catalog, indicates machine time will become an important cost factor that must be considered.

Finally, in evaluating any programming language it is necessary to determine the availability of that language for a variety of machines. Assembly languages fare poorly on this score because they are invariably tied closely to the particular hardware for which they are implemented. A library using assembly language programming is almost certainly faced with major reprogramming costs whenever they change computers (or when the computer center they are using changes computers). Reprogramming is not only costly, it is also time-consuming. Should the reprogramming effort lag behind the schedule set up for the machine change (as frequently happens), vital library services may be severely curtailed during the changeover.

Much the same difficulty awaits a librarian who elects to use a higher-level language directly suited to his needs, but not yet widely available on a variety of machines. Only FORTRAN, COBOL, and ALGOL can be said to be almost universally available in the world of computers. (ALGOL is a scientific language more widely used in Europe than in this country, but generally available on most American equipment.) Initially, this restriction of only a few languages being generally available came about because of the high cost of implementing a language on a given machine together with the general reluctance of programmers to change languages unless an order of magnitude improvement in utility was promised.

Two mediating influences are at work today: the costs of implementing new languages have decreased sharply, and language designers have taken to the approach of extending existing languages to include new facilities, thus minimizing the programmer-retraining problem. For a time there was a hope that a truly general-purpose language would come into being, but this hope generally died with the introduction of PL-1, a language designed (roughly) to coalesce the important attributes of FORTRAN and COBOL and add some of the character manipulation of SNOBOL (discussed below). The generally prevailing view today is that PL-1 attempted too much at the cost of greatly increased implementation cost, loss of operating speed, and restriction (because of the size of the compiler) to rather large machines.

A somewhat different approach that is gaining favor today is the design of a pyramid of macros (sets of assembly code instructions that can be conveniently used as if they were higher-level instructions) with a small base that can be economically converted to a new machine when necessary. Such a system has the nice added feature which allows new operations, as they become useful, to be embedded in the language without redoing the entire system, thus providing the extendability that is now thought necessary for almost any language. The first linguistically oriented macro language was TEMAC and the present version of SNOBOL (version IV) is now implemented in terms of a set of macros.

In sum, a librarian considering the choice of a programming language today has a difficult decision: no existing language scores high on all of the crucial characteristics we have enumerated. Recognition of the fact that his choice may well involve order-of-magnitude changes in his over-all cost picture is a necessary first step. Beyond this the librarian must consciously choose between the advantages and disadvantages of the various routes open to him. In this context, Table 2 may be helpful.

2.4. The Cost of Hardware

Computer hardware, like computer software, was not initially designed for use in the library. The earliest computers were research tools, designed and operated in laboratories for scientific computation. As such, their costs were generally borne by research grants and their usage correspondingly restricted, even in the scientific world. As late as 1951 well-informed scientific leaders were of the opinion that something in the order of ten large scientific machines would be sufficient for the needs of science almost indefinitely. Although much has been made of this historic underestimate of the future, little has been said of the mechanism that served to undermine it. What happened during the decade of the 1950's was that one large company after another saw the utility of the digital computer as a tool for processing financial data. Machines were acquired principally to put out the payroll. This could be done in a very few hours of machine time each week and still pay for the machine. For all practical purposes, the rest of the machine time was free.

The scientific community was not long in recognizing that their experience in mathematical computation could be put to good use. In short, the business community was paying for computation but was also eager to see that such expensive equipment did not stand idle. The scientific community had the "know-how" and the problems to keep the machines busy. Both prospered. By the late 1950's science had demonstrated that it could make use of vast quantities of computer time effectively, and in the present decade most scientific computation is self-supporting.

In considering the use of computers, and particularly in considering the question of leasing time from other centers or buying or leasing a machine directly, librarians would do well to consider the experience of the scientific community. There are few libraries today that have progressed sufficiently in their automation to justify purchase or lease of their own machine. However, that day is not far off for many larger libraries. Much

Table 2   Characteristics of Available Higher-Level Languages

Language	Prime Area of Application*	Relative† Speed	Availability
FORTRAN	Scientific	1/2.0	Complete
ALGOL	Scientific	1/2.0	Almost complete
COBOL	Business	1/2.5	Almost complete
PL-1	Scientific/Business	1/2.5	Large IBM only
SNOBOL IV	Literary	1/10	Most large machines
ALTEXT	Literary	1/1.1	IBM only
Assembly language	All	1/1	Complete but different for each machine

*Application area is to be taken in the context of this study. SNOBOL has been widely used as a teaching tool, an experimental device for building compilers, and for certain scientific problems involving logical matching. ALTEXT also has certain nice features in business applications.

†Relative speed is highly dependent on application. These figures are approximations based on a few experiments in the linguistic processing area only.

of the truly significant breakthroughs in the library are bound to come when libraries have their own equipment with a significant amount of "free" machine time available for experimental work.

Another general point can be gleaned from the historical development of computation. The machine costs of computation have gone down steadily since the first introduction of computers. Figure 9 shows the growth in the number of computations per second over the last 15 years (data are based on a study made in Reference 4). The points appear to lie on three straight lines corresponding roughly to the first, second, and third generations of computers. The striking conclusion from this data is that not only does one find an exponential growth in the number of computations per dollar, but one also notes that each new generation of computers has provided an increased rate of growth! Thus the first generation machines doubled their capabilities every 25 months, the second every 13 months, and the third every 9 months. Presumably, these rates must begin to taper off soon, but as of 1966 no sign of a turndown had yet manifested itself.

In this context, the following observation takes on some significance: a given aspect of library activity can be economically automated at a given time if there is some trade-off of machine time for manpower costs. Once the point of equal trade-off is reached, automation can only look good from here on: subsequent machine costs will go down and subsequent

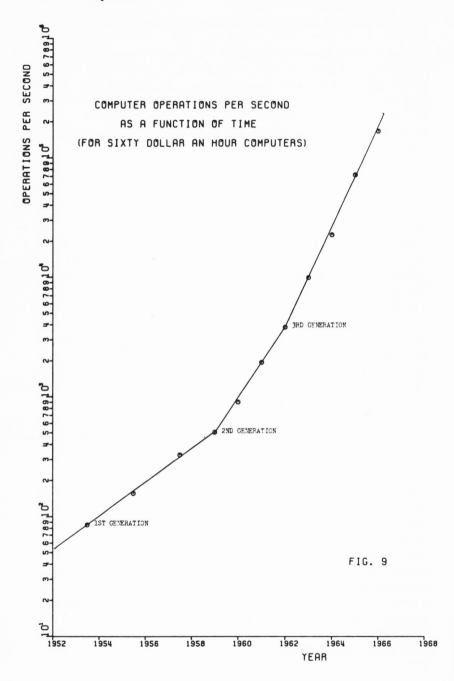

COMPUTER OPERATIONS PER SECOND
AS A FUNCTION OF TIME
(FOR SIXTY DOLLAR AN HOUR COMPUTERS)

3RD GENERATION

2ND GENERATION

1ST GENERATION

FIG. 9

personnel costs will almost inevitably go up (assuming a continuing pros-
perity in the economy). This growing advantage from the machine point
of view is further amplified by the fact that libraries are generally growing
exponentially. Precise calculation of this effect depends on a number of
factors and is further complicated by the fact that machine costs tend to
drop in quantal jumps rather than on a smooth curve. However, libraries
tend to be long-lived organizations by comparison with many of our other
institutions, and any computation of operation costs should include future
projections as well as first-year cost figures. Information on how to
calculate library growth rates is provided in Chapter 5 of this report.
Information on the general growth of salaries and on the growth of salaries
in the library profession is readily available.

As an example, suppose a given library is growing at the rate of 5 percent
per year; its salary structure in the appropriate labor categories for the
trade-off with machine use is growing at the rate of 7 percent per year; and
the average decrease in machine costs is 33 percent per year. Then the
difference in costs per thousand dollars in total cost at the beginning of
the operation, assuming parity at the beginning of the period, is shown in
Table 3.

The quantal jump characteristics of the machine costs changes are such
as to inhibit early growth as compared to that shown in Table 3. However,
the percentage figures we have chosen are conservative and the over-all size
of the change is sufficient to make the point: long-term computations are
necessary to put things in perspective.

Pinpointing the specific areas where machine costs are most likely to
change over the next 5 years involves a certain risk. Recent developments
lead us to believe that the following summary errs on the conservative side.

Output Printers

Until recently, the printing of book catalogs from machine-readable data
was possible only in two modes: the line printer (either upper case only or
upper/lower case at greatly reduced speed) or photocomposition at several
times the costs. Within the past year, electronic composition machines
have begun to appear on the market. Although they are not generally
available to librarians at this time, some libraries have access to them, and
within the coming year most libraries will be able to make use of them on
a service center basis. A thorough summary of photo- and electronic composition equipment is given in Reference 7, albeit without costs. The
summary in Table 4 is based on an article in the *Wall Street Journal* (26
June 1968) covering the *Print 68* show in Chicago.

Table 3   Potential Savings Due to Automation

Year	Cost difference per thousand dollars of initial operation cost
0	$ 0
1	420
2	772
3	1191
4	1353
5	1623
6	1895
7	2178

Table 4   High-Speed Electronic Composition Devices

Type	Char/Sec	Price
(Mergenthaler) Linotron 1010	1000 to 10,000	$400,000
(RCA) Videocomp 70-830	6000	$300,000
(Harris-Intertype) Fototronic-CRT	1100	$300,000 to 500,000

The fastest of these machines (operating at typewriter quality rather than graphic arts quality) is the Linotron 1010. This machine costs approximately three times as much as a standard line printer. However, in its fast mode it operates approximately five times as fast as the fastest line printer operating with upper case only. It gains roughly another factor of three when compared to a line printer operating with upper and lower case. When comparing quality for quality (and ignoring the larger character set of the Linotron), the cost of printing favors electronic composition by a factor of five to one, whereas a year ago comparison with line-printer and photo composition favored the former by at least five to one. Thus the line printer has gone from a five to one favorite to a five to one underdog in a year.

(The trade-off between graphic arts quality and throughput speed involves a number of factors, including the size of the print run for the catalog. This problem is discussed in greater detail in Chapter 3.)

Mass Storage

Another important area of current change is in the cost of mass storage. It is difficult to provide a direct figure on the rate of improvement in this area because this represents a change in kind rather than in degree. From the early 1950's until about 5 years ago, the standard computer configuration consisted of a small internal, high-speed storage (which for the last ten years has been implemented in terms of magnetic cores) and lower cost external memories provided by the use of magnetic tapes and tape readers. The cost of core has gone steadily down, and the cost of tapes and tape readers has also gone down, particularly when the higher operating speeds and higher densities of information per inch of tape are taken into account.

In this context, operations with large files of information were pretty much limited to sequential processing: the information was stored on magnetic tape, read into the machine, and the derived information output on another magnetic tape. The cost of running through a very large file from beginning to end to find one or two items was prohibitive.

However, due largely to the needs of the information retrieval community, there has been a growing demand for inexpensive mass storage where it would be possible to access a handful of points, or perhaps even a single point, in the store without incurring the cost of scanning the entire store (such access is somewhat inaccurately referred to as *random access*). The mechanical procedures for accomplishing this were known from early days in computing, but the lack of demonstrated need inhibited their use except in specially built configurations.

By 1963, a number of large computer installations began adding massive magnetic drums and magnetic discs in their systems, and the successful use of these devices led to their general inclusion in the so-called "third-generation" computers introduced in 1965 and now generally prevailing throughout the industry. The capabilities of these devices are summarized in Table 5.

The question of where these devices will find use is open to some speculation. There are those who feel that eventually the cost of mass storage and access will be so low as to inhibit the need for printed catalogs altogether. This is certainly not the case now and in our opinion it is more likely that for the forseeable future interrogation of mass storage will be limited to a relatively small percentage of all catalog interrogations (perhaps 20 percent at most) and that most of the requests for information will be serviced by printed catalogs.

Be that as it may, the existence of mass storage will tend to make

Table 5 Cost of Mass Storage

Source	Type	Price Rental	Purchase	Size (Million Bytes)	Access Time (Milliseconds)	Transfer Rate (Bytes/Sec)
IBM (International Business Machines)	1) DRUM #2303	$ 410/mo	$ 18,430	3.91	8.6	303.8K
	1) DISC #2311	$ 590/mo	$ 24,510	7-1/4	75	156K
	2) DATA CELL #2321 (Data Cell Attachment #2321)	$2885/mo	$132,400	400	175-600	56K
	#2841 CONTROL UNIT (for 2311/ 2321/2303 DRUM)	$ 180/mo	$ 6,790			
	3) DISC #2314 (All 1 unit— contains control unit & 8 drives)	$ 540/mo $5410/mo	$ 26,430 $244,440	233	75	312K
	1) TAPE UNIT #2415 (Rewind time—4 min)	$ 775/mo	$ 35,650		32	15K (800 bytes/in density)
	#2420 (Rewind time—1 min) (Model 7—automatic threading etc)	$1050/mo	$ 54,600		3	320K (1600 bytes/in density)

*A byte is IBM's term for the amount of storage necessary for one character

Source	Type	Price Rental	Price Purchase	Size (Million Char)	Access Time (Milliseconds)	Transfer Rate (Char /Sec)
CDC Control Data Corp.	1) DISC DRIVE					
	#853	$ 350/mo	$ 15,500	4.1	30-165	208K
	#854	$ 520/mo	$ 23,000	8.2	30-165	208K
	2) DISC FILE					
	#813	$3450/mo	$147,000	100	25-110	196K
	#814	$5500/mo	$241,500	200	25-110	196K
	#3234 CONTROL UNIT (for 853/854/813/814)	$ 540/mo	$ 25,000			
	3) DISC DRIVE					
	#6638 (All 1 unit—built in controller & dual access)	$9400/mo	$325,000	167	25-110	1.68 million
	1) TAPE UNIT #3228 (1X4 tape controller)	$ 445/mo	$ 21,000			
	#3624 (4X16 tape controller)	$4100/mo	$194,500			

significant cost reductions in a number of the possible uses of the catalog. Sorting costs are likely to go down, though present experience is too limited to make precise estimates. Cataloging costs may well be reduced if the cataloger has rapid and inexpensive access to the catalog information. Editing costs will almost certainly be reduced through the use of on-line access on a time-shared basis. Certain more sophisticated operations will become economically feasible through the reduced costs of storing dictionaries, thesauri, and authority lists in the machine for rapid access by a user on-line or through a computer program.

Tape Costs

Experienced users of computing equipment have learned over the years to be wary of recently announced products that have not been in production long enough to ensure a steady supply of reliable pieces of equipment. However, one manufacturer has recently announced its intent to provide very inexpensive input/output equipment designed to read standard magnetic tape cartridges such as are being used in home tape recorders. If this equipment proves effective, it may well have a substantial impact on library automation and particularly on the exchange of machine-readable data between libraries. The total investment in magnetic tapes in many computing concerns is large, not only involving an investment in the tapes themselves but also in the storage space needed and in the access time to locate a tape.

Reduction in the size and cost of magnetic tapes would reduce over-all costs noticeably with consequent savings to all concerned. The further advantages of reduced mailing expenses will not be lost on librarians concerned with interlibrary loans. For comparative purposes, Table 6 provides the basic characteristics of standard computer tape with the new cartridges just announced.

Table 6   Comparison of Home Cartridge Tape and Standard Computer Tape

Home Cartridge Tape	Standard Computer (Mag) Tape (Reels)
300 to 1200 ft reels	600 to 2400 ft reels
128 8-bit char/inch	800 to 1600 bits/inch
1250 char/sec	160,000 char/sec
$4 to $12	$8.75 to $28
4-in. to 8-in. diameter	7-1/2-in. to 11-1/2-in. diameter

Parallel Search Logic

In the early stages of catalog automation, existing hardware and software are sufficient to accomplish the desired tasks inside the computer in the amount of "computer time" available while the machine is reading and writing the data. As greater sophistication is required, the librarian can lean on more efficient software to increase the effective amount of computer time available to him. However, eventually he will require even faster computing equipment to implement complex scanning and matching operations that go along with proper linguistic exploitation of his catalog data.

To a degree, the librarian can depend on the historic process in the development of computers that has produced faster and faster machines at lower and lower costs. There is one other avenue of potential gain available to him. For some years, computer designers and computer users have talked of the possibility of "parallel computers," machines that are capable of carrying out many computations simultaneously in much the same manner as the human brain. It would be a hazardous process at best to predict a reasonable date for the arrival of such equipment in commercially available systems.

However, it is possible to accomplish certain well-specified operations that are to be "built in" to existing equipment or designed into new equipment. It is in this sense that the actual computing logic takes on the peculiar flavor that leads one to think of a given machine as a "business" machine or a "scientific" machine. For instance, in almost all computing it is necessary to be able to determine whether a given number is positive, negative, or precisely zero. In recognition of this, almost all computers have built-in logic that operates at very high speed to make such decisions.

Most machines are evaluated first in terms of their "cycle" time (the minimum time necessary to do anything) and then in terms of the number of cycles necessary to accomplish a given task. Suppose, for instance, that one wished to determine whether a given character were a vowel or a consonant. One way to accomplish this on almost any machine is to store the vowels in the machine and then sequentially match the given character with the store characters one by one. A match at any time would then provide the information that the character was a vowel. If all matches failed, the logic would then conclude that the given character was not a vowel. In a very elementary machine the sequence for a given match would go roughly as follows: (1) the given character would be read into the accumulator; (2) the first of the stored vowels would be read into the accumulator in a negative mode; (3) the accumulator would be tested to see if it were zero; (4) if the value were not zero (i.e., no match had occurred), a counter would be incremented to provide the necessary information that another operation had been completed; (5) the counter would then be tested to see if all the stored vowels had been used as yet; if not, the process would be repeated. Thus, if we were testing against five vowels and no match occurred it would be necessary to do this five-step operation five times. If each step of the operation took just one cycle, the entire operation would take 25 cycles.

A skillful programmer, recognizing this and anticipating repeated use of this kind of operation could easily cut the number of steps in half or more. However, if the machine designer anticipated repeated use of such an· operation for his customers he could build in the entire operation so that it could be accomplished in one or two cycle times, thus providing an order of magnitude improvement in performance.

This is precisely what is done in machine design today. Using whatever information is available to them, machine designers build in a collection of operations that they believe will be useful to whole sets of customers. To take advantage of mass production economies, they will adopt a particular set of options as to what is built in the hopes of being competitive with other machines over the entire computing market.

Many current machines have as standard features, or extra cost options, the capability to compute logarithms, trigonometric functions, and the like in one or two cycle times. None, to our knowledge, can determine whether a given character is a vowel in one or two cycle times. Nor will they until such time as it is quite obvious that there are a significant number of customers who will obtain substantial benefit from such options. Thus where the hardware changes noted earlier in this section are already in the process of happening, the development of specific internal logic for processing linguistic records depends almost entirely on the machine users (in this case, librarians) to analyze their own problems in sufficient detail so as to determine what new internal features would provide order of magnitude savings in computer cost in their operations. It will take time for librarians to find this out and to agree on the features that offer the greatest potential time benefits for them. It will take time for this information to filter back to the machine designers and for the design and implementation of the logic in commercially available equipment. However, given the potential size of the library market not only in public and university libraries, but also in the many librarylike activities in business and industry, it does not seem unreasonable to predict that within the next decade order of magnitude gains will be available in this area.

2.5. The Conversion Problem

User cost factors and the steadily improving picture in hardware and software costs, together with the steadily rising cost of library personnel, will almost certainly force most libraries to an ever-increasing amount of automation. The central role of the catalog in any library operation suggests that no library maintaining a manually operated catalog can be said to be automated in a meaningful sense.

However, any library with a substantial existing catalog must face the formidable barrier of converting that catalog to machine-readable form. Where user costs do not appear in the budget and computer costs are downstream and hold their real promise 3 to 5 years ahead, the cost of conversion is now. Furthermore, conversion is a massive task involving many small decisions at the detail level: what is to be included in the record entry, how is it to be coded, should preediting be used, are cards, paper tape, or OCR better input methods, should the job be done in house or be farmed out, and so on. Few people enjoy the task of facing up to such a myriad of decisions. Once these decisions have been made, there is a substantial amount of detailed supervision required, massive proofreading operations, dislocation of catalog (or shelf list) cards, and siphoning off of many hours of key library personnel from their regular duties. And few libraries are blessed with extra staff.

It is small wonder then that conversion has occupied the central position in much of the literature on catalog automation. It is not the key economic issue in the long run that will determine whether or not a library decides to automate its catalog operation. It is simply a dirty job involving a large one-time cost that provides a substantial stumbling block that must be hurdled before the substantive gains of automation can be achieved.

Supposing that it has been decided that the catalog should be automated, there remains the question of what portion, if any, of the retrospective catalog should be converted, and on what time schedule. The answer will depend on the nature of the library involved. A small public library concentrating heavily on current literature may well decide that much of the retrospective catalog is concerned with materials that will be purged over the next 5 years. Purging involves subjective decision-making on the part of the librarian. The same process can be applied to selecting out the records of items with anticipated long life for inclusion in the main catalog. The cost of applying such a selection procedure will depend critically on local parameters: the way the local catalog is organized, whether new accessions lists have been maintained and include sufficient materials for catalog entries, the salary of the librarian required for the selection process, the cost of duplicating records, and so forth. Hence, such a procedure might be quite attractive for some libraries and very inefficient for others.

Selecting items for inclusion in the catalog in a library with substantial archival collections is basically not sound. Archival collections, almost by definition, are not purged, though subsets of the collection may occasionally be moved to less accessible locations where usage rates are low. In such a collection, one must decide first whether the retrospective material is to be converted and if so on what time scale. It is occasionally put forth that conversion of retrospective materials, particularly in rapidly growing fields such as science, is not necessary. Even if this were so (and few scientists would casually dismiss the prospect of improved access to the traditional literature of their fields) it is hard to believe that many librarians would deny social scientists, historians, or students of language and literature the opportunity to bring modern machine methods to bear on the historical developments in their respective fields. Some of the potential of this approach is discussed in Chapter 7 of this report.

Various strategies exist for breaking down large catalogs into subsets of manageable size so as to minimize dislocation to library staff and operations and to stretch out the entire conversion task over a period of time where budgetary requirements demand this (Refs. 6 and 7). It is unlikely that stretching out the operation will materially affect the cost of conversion in a general sense because the conversion procedure contains both human and machine elements and, as noted previously, human costs tend to increase as machine costs decrease. In a particular library, local conditions will have a strong effect as availability of trained personnel, equipment, and service bureaus,[1] change with time, and these conditions may well not balance out so that delay will be fortuitous in some circumstances and costly in others.

2.6. The Cost of Conversion

A number of studies of conversion costs have been published. Five of these are sufficiently compatible to provide a clear picture of the basic cost structure. All studies assumed use of keypunch equipment.

1. *Los Angeles County Public Library (LACP)*—An *a priori* study of five different methods of input for catalog conversion now in progress (Ref. 8).

2. *Ontario New Universities Library Project (ONULP)*—A pilot study on the cost of catalog conversion based on actual costs of converting 5220 records (Refs. 9 and 10).

3. *University of California/Berkeley (UC/B)*—An *a priori* study based on random samples of catalog information and a set of cost equations previously tested on the Stanford Undergraduate Catalog (Refs. 3 and 11).

---

[1]A *(computer) service bureau* sells computer services to the general public.

4. *Columbia-Harvard-Yale Medical Libraries (CHY)*—A survey of actual production costs at Yale where the end product is a set of catalog cards rather than a printed catalog (Refs. 12, 13, and 14).

5. *Stanford Undergraduate Library (SUL)*—A report on the costs of the first year of operation of a computerized catalog consisting of 25,000 entries (Refs. 3 and 13).

The cost breakdowns as provided from these studies are summarized in Table 7. Various modifications of the published figures were made to obtain a higher degree of compatibility. Because of the widely varying methods of computing overhead, or burden, all costs associated with overhead were eliminated. Several projects made use of the new IBM 1401 computer but at somewhat differing unit costs. These figures were reduced to an equivalent $30/hour rate. The CHY data was reported on a "per catalog card" basis with the note that cards were produced in sets of nine, so that the CHY figures were multiplied by a factor of 9. Some detail information was elicited through communication with the various projects. Where costs were lumped in the various studies, the lumped figures are given using brackets to associate the factors (and in one case a footnote).

In addition, there are individual anomalies that tend to distort the picture slightly. In the ONULP study, all costs connected with the study are included (except for subsequent sorting and manipulative operations on the IBM 7094 which are not considered here). This tends to inflate two of the ONULP figures. The rental figure includes full rental for keypunching equipment used regardless of its utilization on the project. All other figures shown are apparently based on 100 percent utilization costs. Although we have discounted this in the computation of composite costs it is well to note that failure to obtain full utilization of equipment can lead to substantial increases in cost that may overshadow modest differences between different types of equipment. The cost figure for "supplies" is here shown under "punch cards and coding sheets." In the ONULP data this figure includes other supplies such as purchase of magnetic tapes which are not considered in the other studies. Inclusion of the figure here serves as a useful warning: magnetic tapes are costly, and maintenance of a large library of tapes of different orderings of the information will lead to a substantial cost.

The computer time included under "Conversion & List" and "Edit Lists" for SUL is high, though not materially higher than the figures for LACP and ONULP. Two factors are at work here. The 1401 computer used in these three studies can produce a listing of the catalog for editing

Table 7 Comparative Conversion Costs per Title

	1968 LACP 450 char.	1964 ONULP 400 char.	1966 UC/B 317 char.	1964 CHY 243 char.	1966 SUL 180 char.	Composite 425 char.	Estimates 250 char.
Coding/editing	—	—	$0.0803*	—	$0.0440	$0.08	$0.04
Keypunch	>$0.4800	$0.3065	0.1876	$0.1980	>0.1833	0.33	0.17
Rekey	0.1272		0.0304			0.08	0.04
Proofing	0.0840	>0.2586	0.0851	>0.1170	0.1028	0.18	0.10
Rental		0.6503†	—	0.0360	0.0370	0.08	0.04
Conversion & List	0.0200	>0.0957	0.0199	0.0237	>0.1200‡	0.02	0.02
Edit Lists	0.0840			—		0.08	0.04
Punch Cards			—	—	0.0125	0.02	0.01
Coding Sheets	>0.0360	>0.5076§	—	—	0.0208	0.03	0.02
						$0.90	$0.48

*Includes provision for keypunch rental, and supplies

†Full keypunch rental absorbed by pilot project

‡Includes use of automatic error-detection routines

§Includes cost of magnetic tapes and other supplies

purposes as a by-product of the card-to-tape conversion process *if* the user of the list is satisfied with uppercase only output (as is the case in the UC/B data). However, LACP, ONULP, and SUL all produced (or plan to produce) edit lists in upper and lower case. Presumably the utility of this step is to be found in its superiority in checking for errors. In other words, costs of edit lists as included in Table 7 should be attributed to the cost of quality. In the SUL system, automatic error-detection methods were used, and the inclusion of the routines to accomplish this may account for the slightly higher SUL cost for edit lists. In this connection, it is also useful to note that the SUL costs of proofing and rekeying appear to be higher than those for CHY and UC/B, particularly if one takes into account the fact that SUL had a substantially smaller average record length than CHY and UC/B. In part this may be attributed to the inclusion of automatic error-detection routines: the fact that more errors are detected leads to greater correction costs. The cost of quality is substantial, and though none of the studies explicitly identify all the quality costs, nor measure them against known quality performance figures, the user of this information should recognize the existence of these costs and the need to prepare for them in terms of the quality desired. Of the various cost figures involved in conversion, there appears to be less available on quality costs. (Further discussion of methodology in this direction is given in Chapter 4 of this report.)

The nice spread of record size over these five studies (180, 243, 317, 400, and 450 characters, respectively) suggests the possibility of an equally nice set of curves representing the cost breakdown as a continuous function of record size. Unfortunately, the vagaries of the data and the other differences in the projects involved are too great to permit such precise estimation. The two studies (LACP and ONULP) using long records provide good agreement and the three studies using the shorter records provide good agreement. However, the UC/B data (317 characters) agrees better with the SUL data (180 characters) than with the ONULP data (400 characters). This suggests that the better arrangement of the information is to provide two sets of composite figures, the one representing an average of the two studies using 400 characters or more per record (and averaging 425 characters per record), and the other representing an average of the three studies with shorter records (averaging 250 characters per record). These composite figures are given in the last two columns of Table 7. *These figures are to be taken as a convenient summary of the available data, not as a prescription for standard costs.* The number of variables in even as well-defined an operation as data conversion is so great as to prohibit the construction of a set of equations that will apply across all libraries. (However, model cost equations are given in References 3 and 8.)

This is not to suggest that the individual librarian should avoid preparing careful cost estimates. Conversion of a retrospective catalog will represent a substantial portion of any library's budget over the 2 or 3 years it would take to accomplish this in most mature libraries. Those concerned with making decisions as to policy and administering the over-all cost function of the library will properly want carefully prepared estimates of any major cost item. The variability of the data of Table 7 should be a sufficient argument to put the computation of costs in a reasonable perspective.

Two other observations may be of some value. The cost per character for the two composite figures is not identical. For the 250 character column, the total cost is $0.48 per title, or 0.192 cents per character per title. For the 425 character column, the total cost is $0.90 per title, or 0.212 cents per character per title. Given the over-all precision of the data, this is not a significant difference. The sign of the difference does suggest that the complexity of handling longer titles may lead to cost increases beyond those predicted by the length of the record itself. Those contemplating conversion of long record catalogs should be advised that there is at least a suggestion here that costs rise more than linearly.

Finally, in the two composite estimate columns of Table 7 we have included figures for all elements of cost. In some contexts it will be possible to do away with the coding/editing cost and keypunch the data directly from existing documents such as standard catalog cards. In other contexts it will be possible to do without the edit lists. Shortcutting these two operations may lead to undesirable results from the quality point of view, and the effect of this must be adjudged in the context of the given operation. Where it is possible to eliminate both of these steps, the total cost per title will be reduced by approximately 17 percent.

Since the original collection of information reported on in Table 7, the Library of Congress has released detailed information on the cost of converting MARC records (see Simmons, P.A., "An Analysis of Bibliographic Data Conversion Costs," *Library Resources & Technical Services,* 12 (Summer 1968), 296-311). The most recent cost information on this project (kindly supplied in advance of publication by Mrs. Henriette Avram) provides excellent figures on supervision costs (18.3 cents/record) that were not available in the other studies. The MARC figures are also based on the use of a paper tape input typewriter and thus provide us for the first time with a direct comparison of this machine with the punched card equipment. The MARC records have an average character count of 446 characters and hence are most directly comparable to our figures for 425 characters. The summary is shown in Table 7a. The agreement between the two sets of figures for the noncomputer costs is excellent. The MARC

Table 7a   Comparison of MARC Conversion Costs Composite Estimates

	1968 MARC 446 Char.	Composite Estimate 425 Char.
Coding/Editing	$0.17	$0.08
Keying	0.21	0.33
Rekey	0.03	0.08
Proofing	0.13	0.18
Rental	0.16	0.08
Other	0.08	0.05
Noncomputer Costs	$0.78	$0.80
Computer Costs	0.36	0.10
Total Costs	$1.14	$0.90

project had higher initial coding and editing costs and higher keying instrument rental costs. However, these costs increases were offset by reduced keying and rekeying costs, as might be expected.

The MARC computer costs are high. This is explained in part by the need to sort the MARC records for subsequent use and in part by the relatively high printing expense brought on by the need to proofread diacritics, boldface, etc.

2.7.   Comparative Input Equipment Costs

One of the continuing questions in any data processing operation is the question of what keying equipment should be used. There is a growing sentiment that the keypunch is dying (Ref. 6), there is the continuing resistance to the use of punch paper tape in most computer centers together with the continuing experience of almost everyone that keying on a paper-tape typewriter is faster than on a keypunch, and there is increasing enthusiasm for the use of optical character recognition equipment (OCR). Given that a keyboard is a piece of hardware and that hardware costs can, and do, change drastically, the safest observation is that the situation will be different a year or two from now. However, two recent studies (Refs. 8 and 17) help to put the problem in perspective for the time being. The data from these two studies is given in Table 8.

The LACP data is taken from the study previously referred to but with the edit listing costs removed to make it comparable to the other study. The MSU data is from a study of conversion costs of relatively small records (80 to 90 characters) to be used in an automated circulation system.

Table 8 Comparative Costs of Conversion for Different Types of Input Equipment (Per Title)

	Paper Tape	Punch Cards	OCR	Magnetic Tape	On-Line
LACP	$0.75	$0.78	$0.79	$0.78	$1.94
MSU	0.071	0.066	0.066	–	–

The conclusions are straightforward:

1. The cost of on-line input is still prohibitively high.
2. The costs for punch cards, magnetic tape, and OCR are indistinguishable.
3. The cost of paper tape is slightly higher or lower than punch cards, magnetic tape, or OCR, depending on how costs are allocated; hence it is not significantly different from the other modes.

(Among the difficulties in allocating costs one finds such interesting anomalies as the fact that paper tape typewriters are cheaper to purchase and more expensive to lease than card punching equipment.)

Thus the decision as to what machine to use will depend on other than routine operating costs principles. If the keypunch is to die (and the delivery times available on the West Coast at least suggest that it is still a lively item) it will be for other reasons. There are two factors that may well mitigate towards eventual predominance of OCR:

1. OCR input can be prepared on a standard electric typewriter which can be operated by a trained typist, purchased at the lowest price available among the present alternatives, and used for other tasks. Thus the initial investment is low and risk of underutilization is minimized.

2. OCR technology is new when compared to the long-standing technology of punched card equipment. Thus the possibility of dramatic savings in costs in the near future through equipment improvement is much higher for OCR.

2.8. Summary

The conclusions of this study are based on the following basic observations:

1. It is now technically feasible to automate library cataloging operations.
2. Libraries are expanding exponentially.
3. Personnel salaries are growing exponentially.
4. Computing equipment costs are decreasing exponentially.

Table 9   Quick Reference Table for Calculating Input Costs

Average Nationwide Salaries*

	Week	Year
Manager of Programming	$226	$11,752
Lead Programmer	$203	$10,556
Senior Programmer	$180	$ 9,360
Junior Programmer	$151	$ 7,852
Keypunch Supervisor	$125	$ 6,500
Lead Keypunch Operator	$105	$ 5,460
Senior Keypunch Operator	$ 95	$ 4,940
Junior Keypunch Operator	$ 85	$ 4,420

Supplies

Paper Tape	$1.00	(1000 ft roll)
Cards	$0.78/M	(+ $35 order
Mag. Tapes		chg/order)
(Memorax) }	$8.75	(600 ft reel)
(IBM compatible) }	$16.00	(1225 ft reel)
	$28.00	(2450 ft reel)

Business Automation (June 1968)

Optical Page Readers
Price

Type	Rental	Purchase	Max. Speed chars/sec
CDC-915	$4000	$150,000	370
Farrington-3030	$4000-$5000	$150,000	400

Paper Tape Readers
Price

Type	Rental	Purchase	Max. Speed chars/sec
IBM-1017 (Model 2)	$ 75	$3675	120
[Control Unit 2826]	$ 85	$4350	
IBM-2671	$144	$6500	1000
[Control Unit 2822]	$216	$9700	

Table 9 (continued)

Equipment Cost (Keyboard) February 1968

		Type	Purchase Price	Open-ended lease w/option to buy service included 1-yr. lease	No service contract 5-yr. lease
1)	Friden Flexowriter	Letter Writer (bottom/line)	$2795	$ 90.85 (3.25%/2795)	$ 61.49 (2.2%/$2795)
		Model 2201 (top of line)	$4900	$159.25 (3.25%/$4900)	$107.80 (2.2%/$4900)
2)	Honeywell	Keytape (bottom of line)	$7200	East Coast W. Cst. $148 =$248 +$100	No 5 yr. lease
		Keytape (top of line)	$14,000	$335 =$435 shipping cost from East coast 2000 lbs.	

(Note: Keytape makes it possible to enter computer data directly on magnetic tape from a typewriterlike keyboard.

Table 9 (continued)

	Type	Purchase Price	Open-ended lease w/option to buy service included 1-year lease	No service contract 5-yr. lease
3) Dura	Mark 10 (bottom of line)	$3600	$180 (5%/$3600)	$81 (2.25%/3600)
	Mark 10 (top of line)	$4950	$247.50 (5%/$4950)	111.38 (2.25%/4950)
4) IBM-026	Model 1 (Alpha-numeric)	$3475	$ 60.00	
	Model 2 (Numeric)	$3275	$ 55.00	
	Model 21 (Numeric)	$3400	$ 64.00	
IBM-029	Model 29 (Alpha-numeric)	$3600	$ 69.00	No 5 yr. lease

Table 9 (continued)

	Type	Purchase Price	Open-ended lease w/option to buy service included 1-year lease
5) IBM (Selectric Typewriter	Model 711 (11 in. paper capacity) (8-1/2 in. writing line)	$ 460	$ 15.81 (st lease)
	Model 713 (13-1/2 in. paper capacity) (11 in. writing line)	$ 500	$ 16.89
	Model 715 (15-1/2 in. paper capacity) (13 in. writing line)	$ 520	$ 17.42
6) Mohawk (Incremental Tape Recorder)	Model 1101 (Data Recorder)	$7200	$136.50 ($120 + $16.50 service)
	Model 6401 (Data Recorder)	$8000	$165.00 ($145 + $20.00 service)

Hence, even discounting the advantages (and real cost savings) to the user, the question is not *whether* but rather *when* libraries should automate their cataloging operations.

Resolution of the question of timing will depend strongly on the context of the particular library. Availability of equipment and trained personnel will weigh heavily in such a decision, and the present state of the catalog will be a factor. But in general the most serious cost factor will be the cost of converting the retrospective file compared to the annual budget of the library. Public library systems averaging a number of copies per title will generally have a relatively low investment to make in conversion. The anticipated cost of converting the Los Angeles County Public Library catalog is approximately 2.8 percent of their 1967-68 estimated budget, and the conversion is scheduled to be done over a 2-year period. Although not trivial when compared to growth rate of library budgets (LACPL 1967-68 estimated is 17.5 percent greater than the 1966-67 actual), 1.4 percent per year is a relatively small price to pay for automation.

Large university libraries with substantial archival holdings face a more severe problem. A library with a half million titles and an annual operating budget in the order of a million dollars cannot lightly dismiss an initial cost of roughly a dollar a title, particularly when costs after conversion must still be faced before the library can afford to do away with manual catalog maintenance. In such circumstances, archival libraries must either look for special funding and/or spread out their conversion expense over a period of time. The work at Harvard and at Rochester suggests that good strategies exist for spreading out the work and still obtaining substantial short run benefits for both the library and the library user. With the new cost reductions in computer typesetting, it may soon be feasible for some libraries to write off a substantial proportion of the conversion expense through sale of subject-oriented bibliographies to individual users. Table 9 is a reference table for calculating input costs.

References

1. Fasana, Paul J., "Determining the Cost of Library Automation," *ALA Bulletin* (June 1967) 656-661.
2. De Gennaro, Richard, "The Development and Administration of Automated Systems in Academic Libraries," *Journal of Library Automation* 1 (March 1968) 75-91.
3. Hayes, R. M., Shoffner, R. M., and Weber, D. C., "The Economics of Book Catalog Production," *Library Resources and Technical Services* 10 (Winter 1966) 57-90.
4. Knight, Kenneth E., "Changes in Computer Performance," *Datamation* (September 1966) 40-54; "Evolving Computer Performance, 1963-1967," *Datamation* (January 1968) 31-35.

5. Atkinson, Frank, "Cold Composition on Film and Paper," *Australian Lithographer* (February 1968) [Reprints available in this country through CIS Newsletter, Spring 1968].
6. De Gennaro, Richard, "A Computer-Produced Shelf List," *College and Research Libraries* 26 (July 65) 311-315/353.
7. Richmond, Phyllis A., "Book Catalogs as Supplements to Card Catalogs," *Library Resources and Technical Services* 8 (Fall 1964) 359-365.
8. *Optical Character Recognition Research and Demonstration Project,* Los Angeles County Public Library, 1968.
9. Bregzis, Ritvars, "The ONULP Bibliographic Control System," *Proceedings of 1965 Clinic on Library Applications of Data Processing,* University of Illinois.
10. Bregzis, Ritvars, "The Ontario New Universities Library Project—an Automated Bibliographic Data Control System," *College and Research Libraries* 26 (November 1965) 495-508.
11. Cartwright, K. L., and Shoffner, R. M., *Catalogs in Book Form,* Institute of Library Research/UC-Berkeley, January 1967.
12. Sprenkle, P. M., and Kilgour, F. G., "A Quantitative Study of Characters on Biomedical Catalogue Cards—A Preliminary Investigation," *American Documentation* (July 1963) 202-206.
13. Kilgour, Frederick, "Mechanization of Cataloging Procedures," *Medical Library Association Bulletin* 53 (April 1965) 152-162.
14. Kilgour, Frederick, "Library Catalogue Production on Small Computers," *American Documentation* 17 (July 1966) 124-131.
15. Johnson, Richard D., "A Book Catalog at Stanford," *Journal of Library Automation* 1 (March 1968) 13-50.
16. Lee, Malcolm K., "The Demise of the Keypunch," *Datamation* (March 1968) 51-55.
17. Chapin, R. E., and Pretzer, D. H., "Comparative Costs of Converting Shelf List Records to Machine Readable Form," *Journal of Library Automation* 1 (March 1968) 66-74.

Appendix: A Brief Survey of Some Existing Languages for Linguistic Data Manipulation

COMIT

The COMIT language and system were designed at MIT under the direction of Professor Victor H. Yngve (now at the Graduate Library School of the University of Chicago), and made generally available in 1961. It is intended for nonnumerical procedures such as mechanical translation of natural languages, and its latest version, COMIT II, is available on the IBM 709-7090-7094-7040-7044 family of machines. (This compatibility is achieved by restricting the processor to those instructions common to these five machines.)

Both the language and the translator are markedly unconventional. The language's executable statements are called "rules," and they bear a close but often entirely misleading resemblance to algebraic equations. The COMIT rule

$$* -DER = -THE *$$

means, as might be supposed, that the character string DER is to be replaced within some stipulated context by the string THE. However, the rule

$$* N = 1 + 1 *$$

does not assign the value 2 to a numeric variable N, but in fact replaces an occurrence of the letter N within the workspace by a double N, turning PLANED, for example, into PLANNED.

Perhaps because standard algebraic form has been preempted in COMIT notation for the purpose of calling for character manipulation, calling for computation is somewhat awkward. At least in its original version, COMIT permitted the introduction of numeric values only in the form of subscripts, with the implication that they were ordinal numbers. Where the programmer desired to perform computation for other purposes, he commonly had to resort to the creation of dummy entities whose apparent "subscripts" gave him the numeric symbols he required. A recent announcement indicates that some changes promising an improvement in computational ease have been made in COMIT II. It is not yet clear how substantial these are, but the fundamental structure of the COMIT language precludes the use of standard algebraic notation for computation, and in doing so makes it impossible to call for computation in COMIT in the notation made familiar by FORTRAN, ALGOL, and most other programming languages.

Some set theoretic operations can be performed by using a tagging arrangement. For instance, one can tag each character on input as a 'V' (for 'vowel') or 'C' (for 'nonvowel') and then search the input stream for a single vowel (or nonvowel) character by using an expression of the form $1/V (or $1/C). But a search for a multicharacter vowel string of unknown length (which one might want to write as $/V in COMIT-like notation) is not directly possible although it can be performed by a circumlocution requiring several statements. It is not possible to search for elements belonging to the union or intersection or complement of sets in a natural way and it is effectively impossible to define sets predicatively.

The translator that turns COMIT rules into machine language is not a compiler, which would translate them once only, but an interpreter, which translates each statement, at least in part, every time it is to be executed. This approach has the obvious disadvantage of requiring that a substantial amount of work be repeated many times, with consequently greater expenditure of machine time. There are some applications for which the interpretive approach may well be justified because of the greater potential control it puts into the hands of the user, but it is not at all clear what advantage the COMIT user enjoys in compensation for this greatly increased machine time usage. The COMIT translator is comparable to the conventional compiler, however, in being a closed system; that is, in making no provision for its own extension and modification. There is no way for a user to change any operation provided by COMIT, nor to add any fundamentally new one, without making the kind of profound machine-language level study of the translator that is generally beyond his powers. Such a study would be particularly hard to make in the case of COMIT because the intensely proprietary attitude of its designers has made it difficult to get any documentation on its internal structure and operation. COMIT does not even offer its users the standard last resort of dropping into machine language, since they could not manipulate the data objects formed by that system without much greater knowledge of it than they are permitted to acquire. Such an option would not be easy to use even if the necessary information were provided, however, since the machine language the user would have to employ is an unfamiliar one formed by the intersection of some three or four actual machine languages. For further information on COMIT see References 1-3; for comparative evaluations see References 4 and 5.

SNOBOL

The SNOBOL language and translator, developed at Bell Telephone Laboratories and first publicly reported on in 1964 (Ref. 6), may be considered developments of their COMIT counterparts, and many of the judgments made of that earlier system apply to this one as well. The principal improvements offered by SNOBOL 3 over COMIT lie in increased flexibility of input/output operations and more powerful branching operations. A description of the SNOBOL 4 language has recently appeared in preprint form (Ref. 14). The major differences between this version and its predecessors are that (1) arithmetic expressions are ranked in accordance with the standard precedence conventions, so that abnormal parenthesization is no longer required; (2) there is a wider context permissible for writing functional expressions; (3) pattern-matching facilities have been extended, principally by the introduction of ten specific pattern-valued functions.

Reference 14 is not specific about the availability of floating-point arithmetic, although we understand it is available in the Princeton University implementation. Although SNOBOL 4 is a powerful and useful string processor, it still retains many of the defects of previous versions. As in COMIT, the translator is interpretive in nature and remains closed in the sense given above in the discussion of COMIT, and recourse to machine language is still denied. Arbitrary associative searches are not permitted, so that it would be awkward to search for the Nth occurrence of a letter in a string. It would be difficult to replace repeated occurrences of a character by a single occurrence. There are no facilities for extending core memory to external storage media in case the dynamic allocation of core storage overflows memory limits; the programmer must make explicit provisions for this possibility. While there is a function SIZE whose value on the string 'X' is the number of characters in 'X,' there is no mechanism for counting the number of elements from a specified set that occur in the string 'X'. Renaming of strings involves copying the string contents which is usually wasteful of time and memory. Finally, there is currently no provision for adding to the set of pattern primitives other than direct machine language coding.

References 6, 7, and 14 provide further information on SNOBOL.

LISP

The LISP programming system is based on John McCarthy's paper "Recursive Functions of Symbolic Expressions and Their Computation by Machine" (Ref. 15); its implementation as LISP 1.5 was accomplished at MIT and the LISP 1.5 manual (Ref. 13) appeared in 1962.

The language is awkward and tedious to use; for example, the "Wang algorithm for the propositional calculus," a sample LISP 1.5 program given in Reference 13, requires 78 statements which contain an astonishing number of parentheses. An equivalent SNOBOL 4 program (Ref. 14) requires 35 statements (36 for SNOBOL 3). However, LISP 1.5 is a completely general list structure processing language with an unusually simple internal data object structure and a straightforward although complicated source statement structure. The source statement language, while requiring excessively detailed information, provides great power in the description of recursive processes. Arithmetic is awkward because it must be expressed in Polish prefix notation. Auxiliary memory is not available, which limits LISP 1.5's applicability to large text handling problems. For further information see References 5 and 13.

TEMAC

The TEMAC language and processor, created by M. E. D'Imperio of the Department of Defense during the period 1960 to 1962, were designed with a more definite task and group of users in mind than were the previously described compilers and represent higher level and more specialized tools. The most important differences between TEMAC and those others are its built-in recognition of a hierarchy of linguistic data-objects—the word, sentence, and paragraph—and its ability to manipulate these objects indirectly by reference to their tabulated descriptions rather than by physical duplication and movement of their internal representations. TEMAC's explicit recognition of such objects, plus its much more English-like programming notation, give the user more immediately useful tools for the accomplishment of textual-processing tasks than COMIT and SNOBOL do and produce a listing far more readable and valuable as documentation. TEMAC also surpasses the capabilities of these rivals in permitting users to specify arbitrary collating sequences for the internal representation of alphanumeric characters, thus significantly expediting many searching and comparing operations. The TEMAC processor is a compiler rather than, like COMIT's and SNOBOL's, an interpreter; hence

TEMAC programs should require significantly less machine time than those written in either of these other languages, although actual timing comparisons are not available.

TEMAC does have shortcomings, including several it shares with COMIT and SNOBOL. Chief among these are its failure to provide facilities for unrestricted numerical computation in the generally accepted algebraic notation, and failure to provide for ground-level extension of the language itself by users. Computation is permitted the TEMAC user only within the MOVE statement, which permits him to increment or decrement the variable(s) being moved by a single named or literally specified item. This permits the user, in principle, to perform any desired computation, but only in a manner so unnatural in notation and wasteful in machine time (he will not generally want the result of every addition and subtraction stored in memory) as to make extensive computation impractical. Extendability of the TEMAC language should have been easy to provide, since it is apparently implemented as a body of macros, but no attempt has been made to exploit this advantage. It *is* possible to intersperse machine-language instructions in TEMAC programs and thus create functions not provided in the language, but it would seem that any extensive use of this facility would require a very detailed knowledge of TEMAC's internal operations and organization of data. TEMAC has other more minor disabilities: names of categories must be digits and hence cannot reflect the natural structures being investigated; all dictionary lookup procedures operate entirely in core, seriously limiting the types of problems that can be studied with TEMAC; there is little in the way of set theoretic operations; and there is no sort capability. For further information on TEMAC see References 8 and 9.

ALTEXT

The ALTEXT language was designed by M. R. Stark of Lockheed Missiles & Space Company in 1964-1965 in response to needs for handling linguistic data expressed by J. L. Dolby and H. L. Resnikoff, and was implemented by means of XPOP. XPOP currently runs on the IBM 7094 and can compile ALTEXT programs for either that machine or, at the programmer's option, the IBM 360 (XPOP itself has been largely rewritten as an ALTEXT program, and the part that has been so rewritten has been bootstrapped over to compile on the IBM 360). ALTEXT, by virtue of its manner of implementation, has two important features not possessed by the other languages discussed here: (1) it offers users full computational facilities, both fixed and floating point, in the standard algebraic notation, and (2) it can be extended and modified, both functionally and in notation, by users. The language itself offers some distinctive features. Its most important statements can be used with a variety of degrees of sophistication, reflecting the large number of optional parameters they permit. The nonprofessional user, who is concerned with getting his program running simply and quickly, even at the cost of the highest possible efficiency, can ignore the optional parameters (or may even be unaware of their existence); the more expert programmer can use them to exploit his greater knowledge of the compiler and programming techniques and be rewarded with higher efficiency. ALTEXT's statements are also more like English-language sentences, although their designer by no means used all the XPOP facilities he might have for achieving a "natural" programming language.

The flavor of ALTEXT as a language may be conveyed by a few examples:

a)   SUBSTITUTE A FOR B IN N CHAR AT INPUT, I − 2

This statement will scan the N-character string (where N's value has been computed earlier), starting at the $(I − 2)$th character position of the stream called INPUT, and replace every occurrence of the character "B" within that segment by the character "A."

b) TABLESEARCH PREFIX FOR 3 CHAR AT INPUT 1, IF NO MATCH GO TO GET

This statement compares every entry in the table PREFIX with the first three characters of the stream INPUT, transfers to GET if unable to find a match, to the next statement otherwise.

c)   IF INDEX IS GREATER THAN 8, COPY 71 CHAR AT INPUT 2 TO OUTPUT 41

If the value of the variable INDEX is algebraically greater than eight, the 71 characters starting at the second position in the stream INPUT are copied into the stream OUTPUT starting at its 41st position.

In each of the three statements illustrated, we have selected one—usually the simplest—of their many possible variant forms. Not all their available features have been employed; each of them accepts more parameters than we have actually offered, and many of the parameters we did offer might have been very different had we cared to make them so: simple numbers might have been algebraic expressions, field names might have been literal character strings, and branching directions left implicit (as in example c) might have been made explicit.

Tests have shown that ALTEXT is nearly two orders of magnitude faster than either COMIT or SNOBOL.

The ALTEXT language is not as sophisticated as its competitors, although approximately the same number of statements are required to program a given simple problem in COMIT or SNOBOL. Logical operations are weak and set theoretical operations are mainly accomplished by a (sometimes awkward) table lookup, which, however, is efficient and applicable to very large tables. Predicative set definition is not possible, and operation on symbol strings is possible only by circumlocution. For further information on XPOP see References 10 and 11; for further information on ALTEXT see Reference 12 and its forthcoming revision. The reader is also advised to compare C. Strachey's paper "A General Purpose Macrogenerator" (Ref. 16).

Appendix References

1. Research Laboratory of Electronics/Computation Center, MIT, *An Introduction to COMIT Programming,* Cambridge, Mass.; The MIT Press, 1961.
2. Research Laboratory of Electronics/Computation Center, MIT, *COMIT Programmers Reference Manual,* Cambridge, Mass.: The MIT Press, 1961.
3. Yngve, V. H., "COMIT," *Comm. ACM 6* (March 1963) 83-4.
4. Hsu, R. W., *Characteristics of Four List-Processing Languages,* Washington, D. C.: National Bureau of Standards Report 8163, 1963.
5. Bobrow, D. G., and Bertram Raphael, "A Comparison of List-Processing Computer Languages," *Comm. ACM 7,* 4 (April 1964) 231-240.
6. Farber, D. J., R. E. Griswold, and I. P. Polonsky, "SNOBOL, A String Manipulation Language," *J. ACM 11,* 1 (January 1964) 21-30.
7. Trotter, H. F., *Introduction to SNOBOL—PART I,* Programming Notes Number 31, Princeton University Computer Center, Princeton, New Jersey, 1966.
8. D'Imperio, M. E., *TEMAC (Text Macro Compiler): A Machine Language for Processing Text.* Unpublished working paper, Department of Defense, 1965.
9. D'Imperio, M. E., *TEMAC: A Machine Language for Processing Text. Programming Manual, Part I.* Unpublished working paper, Department of Defense, no date.
10. Halpern, M. I., "XPOP: A Meta-Language Without Metaphysics," *Proceedings of the Fall Joint Computer Conference* (1964) 57-68.
11. Halpern, M. I., *A Manual of the XPOP Programming System,* 3rd ed. (March 1967), Lockheed Missiles & Space Co., Palo Alto, Calif.
12. Stark, M. R., *MPL1 Multiple Purpose Language Manual, Version 1.* (September 1965), Lockheed Missiles & Space Co., Palo Alto, Calif.
13. McCarthy, John, et al., *LISP 1.5 Programmer's Manual,* MIT Press, Cambridge, Mass., 1962.
14. Griswold, R. E., et al., "Preliminary Description of the SNOBOL 4 Programming Language," Reprint, Bell Telephone Laboratories, 6 July 1967.

15. McCarthy, J., "Recursive Functions of Symbolic Expressions and Their Computation by Machine," *Comm. ACM 3* (1960) 184-195.
16. Strachey, C., "A General Purpose Macrogenerator," *Computer J.* (October 1965).

3 The Influence of Typography on the Cost of Printed Catalogs

3.1. Introduction

There are a number of factors affecting the density of information in a printed library catalog. Among these will be the choice of type face, the leading, the format used, the amount of spacing between entries and between columns, and the size of the margin.

The importance of information density stems from the fact that library book catalogs will take up a great number of pages to provide the usual author, title, and subject listings even for relatively small collections. A number of factors affect the cost and the use of such a catalog. From the cost point of view, the more characters per page the fewer the pages and hence the less the cost of paper, printing, and binding. In addition, densely printed catalogs will occupy less shelf space both in the library and in the off-site areas where they will be used, and for those libraries that expect to mail a number of copies to other library centers there will be savings in mailing cost. Finally, though there have not been sufficient studies to enable us to pin this factor down precisely, it seems reasonably clear that the more information per page the more rapidly the user can scan the information.

For these reasons, we will assume in this report that it is desirable to obtain the greatest number of characters per square inch (while maintaining legibility) and will assess the effect of this measure on different type faces and styles for various machines.

3.2. Type Face Design

Computer Line Printer Type Faces

Perhaps the simplest machine to analyze for type face design is the standard computer line printer. Almost all line printers that are generally available today produce a standard pica measure type face; that is, there are a total of ten characters to the inch horizontally and the line spacing is six lines to the inch vertically. (Some machines can be reprogrammed to produce eight lines to the inch but computer centers seldom take advantage of this fact and we will assume here that six lines to the inch is the standard for the industry.)

As a result, a line printer produces 60 characters to the square inch. These characters are uniformly spaced regardless of the character set used: a capital "W" takes up as much space, but no more than, a lower case "i," assuming that a lower case alphabet is available. Generally, italics are not available in standard line printer fonts, but with many machines it is possible to obtain a reasonable approximation to bold face by over-printing the given character. This over-printing slows down the speed of the machine by a factor of two whenever it is in use but does not cause any change in the space taken up by a given message.

Line printer output can be photo-reduced so that higher density output can be obtained. Although there is no general agreement on the smallest size that users are likely to accept, it is rare to find any computer printout that has been reduced by a factor of more than two. Such a reduction would usually be called a 50 percent reduction; however, since it applies to all directions it results in multiplying the number of characters per square inch by a factor of four. Thus line printer output can be said to vary from 60 characters to the inch (as it comes out of the machine) to a maximum of 240 characters to the square inch after 50 percent photo-reduction.

Strike-On Type Faces

With the present speed constraints on mechanically driven typewriters, it is unlikely that anything as large as a library catalog would be produced by typewriter. As the typewriter is a common machine that provides a useful bridge between the line printer and standard printing equipment it is useful to consider this device and the variety of possibilities it presents.

A standard "pica" typewriter will usually produce essentially the same output as a line printer; that is, ten characters to the inch horizontally and six lines to the inch vertically, with uniformly spaced characters. However, several variations are commercially available. The standard "elite" typewriters generally have 12 characters to the inch horizontally. European machines are available with 14 characters to the inch and seven lines to the inch, and it is not impossible to find machines that go as high as 17 characters to the inch and eight lines to the inch. Photo-reduction is, of course, possible with typewriter output as well as with line printer output and it seems reasonable to suggest that a 50 percent reduction from pica and perhaps a 60 percent reduction from elite represent maximum reductions consistent with wide public use.

However, in addition to the variations due to smaller type sizes, one can also obtain typewriters that make use of proportionally spaced characters; that is, such that the horizontal width of the characters differs throughout the character set. Typically, the lower case "i" will be two units wide, whereas the upper case "W" will be five units wide, thus achieving a ratio of 2-1/2 to 1 between the widest and the narrowest characters in the character set. The impact of this can be seen from the following display which shows the same line written first by a standard "elite" typewriter and second by a proportionally spaced typewriter with a reasonably dense spacing. The uniformly spaced material is approximately 14 percent wider than the proportionally spaced material.

Figure 10   Uniform Spacing vs. Proportional Spacing

Modern composition depends on the refreshing chara

Modern composition depends on the refreshing character of

In uniformly spaced material there is no basic difference between printing in all upper case and printing in upper and lower case. However, with proportionally spaced material, it is quite clear that printing in upper and lower case makes a considerable difference. In Figure 11 we see that the same segment of information takes approximately 33 percent more space when printed entirely in caps than it does when it is printed in lower case (with an initial cap).

Figure 11   All Caps vs. Caps and Lower Case

MODERN COMPOSITION DEPENDS ON THE REFRESHIN

Modern composition depends on the refreshing character of

Generally, typewriters do not have the capability to provide italics or bold face character sets, though the double hammering trick used with computer line printers can produce an approximation to bold face with some typewriters. However, the use of double hammering to obtain bold face does not change the amount of space required to print a given amount of information, regardless of whether one is using uniformly spaced or proportionally spaced character sets.

The IBM Selectric Typewriter requires a fixed area for each character although the type font can be changed. Proportionally spaced fonts cannot currently be used by this machine.

Printing Type Faces

As soon as one considers the possibility of using graphic arts quality printing devices, the number of possibilities available for varying the character density is greatly increased. Most graphic arts quality machines will have several character sets: standard (usually called Roman), italics, bold and/or semi-bold, and possibly small caps. In addition, there is a wide range of different sizes available for most character sets. As printers do not generally speak in terms of characters per lineal inch or characters per square inch, it is useful to introduce standard printing terminology in this discussion. Horizontal measurement is generally made in terms of "picas." A pica is approximately 1/6 inch (for the purposes of this discussion we will assume that it is precisely 1/6 inch). Thus a 36-pica line takes up 6 inches of space horizontally. Vertical measurement is normally done in "points." A point is precisely 1/12 of a pica, or approximately 1/72 inch. Hence, a 6-point type will take up 1/12 inch in the vertical direction, or to put it another way, with 6-point type one can print 12 lines to the vertical inch. There are a number of different ways of measuring vertical distances but we will remain with the elementary measures here. As the maximum character density generally used with computer line printers corresponds to a 50 percent photo-reduction that leads to 12 lines to the inch, we will examine the potentialities of graphics arts printing equipment on the basis of a 6-point font.

Almost all graphic arts quality type faces are proportionally spaced, with the attendant savings in space used in the horizontal direction. However, the variation from one type face to another can be considerable and the variation in the use of all caps as opposed to caps or lower case or the use of bold face is significant. We will use a conveniently available type face catalog (*Alphatype*) to indicate what the possibilities are in current composition practice.

Figure 12 contains a typical selection of type faces from the Alphatype catalog. For each type face we have illustrated a line of all caps and another line of caps and lower case. The various type faces have been arranged according to the total number of characters in a given 3.3-inch sample in the Alphatype catalog. The particular sample given in the catalog roughly approximates the monographic letter frequencies for English text. The variations do not appear to restrict the conclusions given below.

One must bear in mind that all of the displays in Figure 12 are 6-point type faces. We observe that the smallest number of characters per horizontal inch corresponds to the use of upper case Versatile Bold: 44 characters appeared in the 3.3-inch wide standard entry. This corresponds to 13.3 characters per inch. At the other extreme, lower case Alphavers Book Condensed provided 89 characters in the 3.3-inch line, corresponding to 27.3 characters per horizontal inch, and hence more than twice the density of the upper case Versatile Bold.

There are a number of other useful observations we can make. First, the 50 percent reduced line printer gives 20 characters to the inch, which is at the margin of acceptable practice. Using the Book Condensed figure given above, we see that the use of all caps leads to 21.2 characters per inch, or approximately 6 percent more than the 50 percent reduced line printer, with a considerable improvement in legibility. Further, if one uses Book Condensed lower case, one obtains 26.9 characters per inch, or approximately 34.5 percent more material per page. In a major library catalog, such as that of the British Museum, which runs to 263 volumes, a saving of 34.5 percent just from a change in type face is a considerable item.

From the information in Figure 12 we can also see that there are reasonably consistent similarities and differences. In the first place, when one compares Roman with italics and semi-bold (or Condensed bold) faces, one finds that for both upper case and lower case the number of characters per inch is the same for each of these standard variations. Bold face, however, generally takes about 7 percent more room than any of the other three.

Equally we find that there is a consistent difference of some 25 percent between the use of caps and lower case, in the favor of lower case, of course. Further, if we compare like things, that is, all caps for Versatile Bold (the most space-using face) to all caps for Book Condensed, we find that there is about a 50 percent increase in character density in using Book Condensed.

In sum, if the primary concern were to pack as much information as possible for a given point size on a square inch of paper, then one should consider the following:

1. Adequate variation in style of face can be obtained by restricting use to Roman, italics, and semi-bold (rather than bold) with no loss of space in either upper or lower case.

2. The use of all upper case is one of the most damaging practices from the viewpoint of maintaining high character density. For any one of the

Figure 12   Selected Alphatype Fonts Arranged According to Increasing Character Density

6 Clarendon Wide
MODERN COMPOSITION DEPENDS ON THE REFRESHING
Modern composition depends on the refreshing character of cui
0123456789$

6 Garamond Bold
MODERN COMPOSITION DEPENDS ON THE REFRESHING
Modern composition depends on the refreshing character of currei
0123456789$

6 Claro
MODERN COMPOSITION DEPENDS ON THE REFRESHING
Modern composition depends on the refreshing character of cu
0123456789$

6 Century Text
MODERN COMPOSITION DEPENDS ON THE REFRESHING
Modern composition depends on the refreshing character of current
0123456789$

6 Alphavers Book
MODERN COMPOSITION DEPENDS ON THE REFRESHING
Modern composition depends on the refreshing character of
0123456789$

6 Caledo
MODERN COMPOSITION DEPENDS ON THE REFRESHING
Modern composition depends on the refreshing character of curr
0123456789$

6 Versatile 45
MODERN COMPOSITION DEPENDS ON THE REFRESHING
Modern composition depends on the refreshing character of
0123456789$

6 Alpha Gothic
MODERN COMPOSITION DEPENDS ON THE REFRESHING
Modern composition depends on the refreshing character c
0123456789$

6 Alphavers Book Condensed
MODERN COMPOSITION DEPENDS ON THE REFRESHING
Modern composition depends on the refreshing character
0123456789$

6 Clarendon Wide Bold
MODERN COMPOSITION DEPENDS ON THE REFRESHING
Modern composition depends on the refreshing character of cur
01234567890

6 Garamond Bold Italic
MODERN COMPOSITION DEPENDS ON THE REFRESHING
Modern composition depends on the refreshing character of curre
0123456789$

6 Claro Italic
MODERN COMPOSITION DEPENDS ON THE REFRESHING
Modern composition depends on the refreshing character of cu
0123456789$

6 Century Text Italic
MODERN COMPOSITION DEPENDS ON THE REFRESHING
Modern composition depends on the refreshing character of current
0123456789$

6 Alphavers Book Italic
MODERN COMPOSITION DEPENDS ON THE REFRESHING
Modern composition depends on the refreshing character of
0123456789$

6 Caledo Italic
MODERN COMPOSITION DEPENDS ON THE REFRESHING
Modern composition depends on the refreshing character of curr
0123456789$

6 Versatile 46
MODERN COMPOSITION DEPENDS ON THE REFRESHING
Modern composition depends on the refreshing character of
0123456789$

6 Alpha Gothic Italic
MODERN COMPOSITION DEPENDS ON THE REFRESHING
Modern composition depends on the refreshing character c
0123456789$

6 Alphavers Bold Condensed
MODERN COMPOSITION DEPENDS ON THE REFRESHING
Modern composition depends on the refreshing character
0123456789$

type faces it is much better to use semi-bold upper and lower case rather than all upper case.

3. There are significant differences among type faces. When planning the printing process a careful study of the type faces available for a given machine should be made before authorizing the use of any particular type face.

3.3. The Effect of Format

The preceding arguments basically refer to character densities for unformatted text, and in this case there is no place for the sole use of upper case characters. It is necessary to introduce a number of format elements in the page design of printed library catalogs, however, so that the introduction of purely upper case characters in selected information fields may sometimes be possible without significantly decreasing the effective information density. In particular, there will be certain justification losses and there also will be a greater use of capitalization in a catalog entry than would normally be encountered in running text samples. Consequently, it is frequently possible to use bold face and pure upper case for certain short elements of the record such as those that occur at the beginning or at the end of an entry where it is in any event necessary to fill out the line to the right margin. Thus the extra space can be "soaked up" by the use of less efficient type styles; occasionally an extra line will be required where the use of the low-density type face will force the line to run over.

To investigate the effects of different formats on character density, we have studied five documents: one public library book catalog, one university library book catalog, one commercially produced bookseller's list, and two telephone directories. One of the last is printed four columns per page; the other is printed five. Telephone directories were chosen for two basic reasons: first, the competing requirements of rapid legibility and small bulk (and hence cost) are unusually acute and quite similar to requirements for library book catalogs, and second, the vast experience of the telephone companies suggest that natural processes of trial and error probably have led to a format compromise that is a good approximation to the ideal.

The primary statistic of interest is the ratio of the number of information-bearing characters to the total number of possible characters on a page, disregarding running heads, pagination, margins, etc. The effects of varying type face size, as discussed above, are essentially eliminated using this ratio; hence it provides a measure of the effect of format alone.

The ratio varies from 49.7 percent for the public library catalog (which was produced in single-column format on EAM equipment) to 78.3 percent for the five-column telephone directory. The lost space—that is, space not devoted to information-bearing characters (interword spaces *are* information bearing in this context in that they delimit word boundaries)—can conveniently be partitioned into four categories: intercolumn space, interentry blank lines, indented lines, and justification losses. The corresponding data are shown in Table 10.

Table 10 makes it clear that increasing the number of columns per page increases the information density. There is, of course, a maximum number of columns that can reasonably be accommodated, but this number will depend on the characteristics of the material to be printed. If the subject material consists of library catalog card contents, then the maximum number of columns will depend on whether a short form of the complete bibliographical reference is used. In any event, the tabulated data for the Bro-Dart catalog shows that telephone directory densities can be approached in the library context.

3.4. Conclusions

One of the essential problems of using book catalogs is the cost of periodically publishing the catalog to include entries for recent acquisitions. The over-all cost of publishing includes the composition cost, the printing and binding costs, and paper costs. Composition costs are rela-

Table 10 Percentage of Space Devoted to Information-Bearing and Non-Information-Bearing Characters

Category	Montogomery County Public Library Catalog (1)*	Stanford Undergraduate Library Catalog (2)	Bro-Dart Catalog of Books (2)	Oakland Telephone Directory (4)	San Francisco Telephone Directory (5)
Information-bearing	49.7%	52.3%	68.5%	76.0%	78.3%
Intercolumn blanks	—	8.3	5.6	1.6	1.9
Interentry blank lines	—	18.5	1.7	2.1	2.0
Indentation losses	11.0	2.6	2.5	0.3	0.7
Justification losses	39.3	18.3	21.6	20.0	17.0

*Numbers in parentheses denote the number of columns per page.

tively independent of format and type size (though this factor varies with different composition devices) and are steadily decreasing as electronic composition devices become more readily available. The printing, binding, and paper costs are primarily a function of the total amount of space taken up by the catalog material. These costs can be minimized by choosing condensed type faces in small point sizes, by restricting the use of all-caps formats, by using semibold type faces in place of bold, and by maximizing the character density per square inch. The various factors are of sufficient importance to enable one to obtain two and three to one publication cost savings through proper choice of type face and format.

4 Efficient Automatic Error-Detection in Processing Bibliographic Records

4.1. Introduction

The increasing use of computing equipment to process bibliographic records in libraries has led to an increased need for efficient detection and correction of errors in such records. Some of the potentially useful methods were discussed in Cox and Dolby (Ref. 1) and Cox, Dews, and Dolby (Ref. 2). However, both of the summaries given in these two references were based on the experience of the authors rather than on a careful enumeration of the particular errors that occurred in practice in the processing of bibliographic records. In this paper we consider the automatic error-detection procedures used in compiler programs to take advantage of the long-standing experience in error-detection developed in this field. We then study errors actually occurring in samples of bibliographic material keyboarded at Harvard (Ref. 3) and Stanford (Ref. 4) Universities to establish a first approximation to the priority that should be given to the various types of procedures in this field.

4.2. Error-Detection in Computer Programs

Perhaps the most detailed work on automatic error-detection in structured data has been carried out on computer programs themselves. A computer program consists of a sequence of instructions each of which is scanned by the machine on input to determine if it is in proper form. A variety of error-checking routines are provided to identify and localize various possible improper representations in the program. Capability to actually correct certain types of errors is generally introduced. One recently developed language (PL1) has something of the order of 1000 error messages of various types. The following messages indicate the type of correction capabilities in one version of PL1 (Ref. 5):

RIGHT PARENTHESIS INSERTED IN STATEMENT NUMBER XXXXX.

IDENTIFIER MISSING IN STATEMENT NUMBER XXXXX. A DUMMY IDEN-
TIFIER HAS BEEN INSERTED.

A LETTER IMMEDIATELY FOLLOWS CONSTANT IN STATEMENT NUMBER
XXXXX. AN INTERVENING BLANK HAS BEEN ASSUMED.

IMPLEMENTATION RESTRICTION. IDENTIFIER YYYYY IN STATEMENT
NUMBER XXXXX IS TOO LONG AND HAS BEEN SHORTENED.

ILLEGAL CHARACTER IN APPARENT BIT STRING YYYYY IN STATEMENT
NUMBER XXXXX. STRING TREATED AS CHARACTER STRING.

TEXT BEGINNING YYYYY IN STATEMENT NUMBER XXXXX HAS BEEN
DELETED.

There are, of course, important differences in the processing of computer programs and the processing of the large lists found in a library
catalog. Computer programs generally consist of a few hundred lines of
instruction, while catalogs must be measured in the tens or hundreds of
thousands of lines. The program compiler must, as a matter of course,
completely unscramble the syntax of the program to make the necessary
translation, although the processing of the catalog requires only as much
unscrambling as is necessary for the task at hand, a task that frequently
requires no more than the identification of the starting point of each field
in the entry.

An error in a catalog entry, although annoying, need not cause a complete rerun. An error in a computer program that is not detected and
corrected by the compiler will, however, usually require a complete rerun.
Thus, one can afford to greatly increase the run time for processing computer programs as long as a corresponding decrease in the number of
reruns occurs. In terms of run times, compilers can and do process as few
as one or two instructions per second. Processing items of large lists must
necessarily be of the order of 50 or more lines per second.

Thus, it does not seem reasonable to establish error-checking routines in
production processes at the same level as the one thousand presently
found in PL1. However, this does not imply that one should necessarily
use less sophisticated techniques. Although no figures appear to have been
published on the efficiency of various routines, it is reasonable to assume
that efficiency will fall off exponentially if the error-checking routines are
ordered by frequency of application. If this is true, the essential problem is
to find those routines that are rich in their ability to detect errors.

At the same time, we must recognize that there are certain types of
errors that can be detected quite easily. That is, the programming sophisti-

cation required is relatively slight and the time to process the information is short. For the moment let us restrict our considerations to transcription errors created by keyboard operators converting a card catalog to machine-readable form. Then such routines can frequently be incorporated even though an analysis of the output would show that they provide relatively little return for a good operator. There are two functions that must be taken care of by the automatic error-detection procedures. For the new operator, who may be less than completely familiar with the format requirements of the system, the capitalization requirements, and so forth, one must provide a rapid feedback of mechanical errors that are easily detected by the machine. This feedback is essential to the over-all quality control operation of which automatic error-detection is only one part. For the well-trained operator who has gotten beyond these naive errors, one needs more sophisticated routines that would be more costly to program or more costly to operate, and it is here that one must make a very careful analysis of the situation to determine which errors will occur with sufficient frequency to make it worthwhile to add the programming and running cost of the more sophisticated error-detection routines.

4.3. Format-Dependent Errors

The errors that are the easiest to catch are those that depend essentially on format; these are the very errors that a new operator might be expected to make more frequently. One of the simplest ways to detect errors is to define, for each field of the record, a set of legitimate codes and then to flag any record that has an illegitimate code by this definition. For instance, in a field devoted to date of publication one might restrict the legitimate codes to numeric values. In most bibliographic records it would be reasonable to go even further and require that the date be a number between 1500 and the present date. In a similar fashion one can specify that the codes available for the author field be the alphabetic code, spaces, and a few marks of punctuation such as the comma and the hyphen. It is also possible to make a list, at the end of each batch of data that is fed into the computer, of all those codes that occur in each position of each field. One can then check back in a subsequent run to determine the forms including the occurrence of very infrequent codes in any of the fields where such infrequent codes occurred.

Another simple check that is almost always worth including is a global check, one that depends upon the fact that the incoming records are given in some natural order, perhaps alphabetic, perhaps numeric, or, if the records are given in class number order, by a mixed alpha-numeric code. It is a relatively simple matter to store the code of each record and compare successive codes to be sure that they are increasing or decreasing as the situation requires and to output error signals any time the given order is violated.

It requires only a slightly further degree of sophistication to check for the use of capital letters in certain fields. For instance, the title information will normally follow certain accepted rules of capitalization. These are not entirely trivial. There are variations from one set of bibliographic records to another, but it is fairly simple to establish the general format describing which words are to be capitalized or which words are not to be capitalized, depending upon the situation, and to check this on input for possible error messages. Under certain circumstances, if the format specified to the machine is not sufficiently sophisticated, some large proportion of the records would drop out with potential error messages. To detect this, one should automatically accumulate the number of each type of error-detection made and print out a summary at the end of the run. Further, if each batch is identified by operator, the summary should reflect this to allow the supervisor of the keyboarding operation to get an immediate check on which operators are producing the most errors and what types of errors are occurring most frequently. The proper feedback to the operators themselves, of course, would then greatly improve the over-all error rate of the system.

It is sometimes argued that automatic error-detection procedures could be so efficient as to make it immaterial how many input errors are generated by the keyboarders. However, as we shall show later in this paper, it is very unlikely that one could economically construct automatic error-detection procedures to handle more than 50 to 60 percent of the incoming errors. Therefore, if the proper quality control procedures are used and the incoming error rate is reduced to a minimum, the number of residual errors left after the automatic error-checking process will in turn be significantly reduced.

One other general category of "simple-to-detect" errors is that having to do with the punctuation and spacing conventions of the record. Such a check must again depend upon the format of the given record, but once the format is specified, it is possible to make a number of relatively simple checks to ensure that spaces are not left out, that double spaces are reduced, that the proper number of spaces follow commas, periods, dashes, and so forth.

Finally, there is a definite correlation between the errors introduced by the keyboarder, and the input material and keyboarding conventions that are established for the system. There does not appear to be sufficient information available today to determine just what would constitute an ideal situation. However, it seems reasonable to maintain that clean input will lead to clean output and that sufficient redundancy should be maintained in the keyboarding conventions to allow checks on the more difficult types of keyboarding. Some hint as to what would be desirable is contained in the analysis which follows.

4.4. Analysis of the Harvard and Stanford Universities Edited Samples

The two samples available to us for this study were kindly provided by Harvard University and Stanford University from the work on the Widener Shelf List and the Meyer Undergraduate Catalog, respectively. Both samples are relatively small but are of sufficient scope to provide some insight into the problem. In each case, after initial keyboarding, the cards were read into an IBM-1401 computer where certain error-detecting procedures were used in the course of reading, formatting, and printing out the data.

The input format used by the keyboard operator differed considerably in these two cases. The Widener Shelf List is a large collection (approximately 1.6 million titles) and is being keyboarded section by section over a lengthy period. The material is contained in manuscript form; hence the keyboarder has to read the manuscript writing, make certain interpretations, and convert these into the keyboard conventions. In addition, there is a significant number of foreign language documents and a conversion problem from the Cyrillic to the Roman alphabet. On the other hand, Widener Shelf List entries are relatively short; approximately 80 percent of the entries can be printed out on a single line of computer output and less than half of 1 percent of the entries require more than two such lines.

At Stanford the situation is quite different. Here a new collection is being extracted from a larger library collection and is added to for the particular purposes of the undergraduate student. Although many of the documents had been cataloged for the main library, a new catalog was produced for the undergraduate library itself, and this was done directly in machine-readable form. The catalog entries were copied onto a particular format specifically designed for the keyboard operator. The Stanford information was more nearly a full bibliographic description than the Harvard information. The Stanford entries typically required four to six lines of computer printout.

Some of these differences showed up in subsequent analysis of the errors occurring in the sample. In each case, after the material had been processed by the computer it was proofread and the necessary corrections indicated on the computer output sheet. These original sheets were made

Table 11 Errors Found in the Harvard and Stanford Edit Lists by Category

Category	Stanford		Harvard	
	No. of Errors	Percent of Total	No. of Errors	Percent of Total
Sequence Errors	40	14	9	5
Missing Information:	99	35	83	49
Codes and Delimiters	46	16	36	21
Spaces	23	8	—	—
Punctuation	13	5	8	5
Capitalization	8	3	26	15
Diacritics	5	2	3	2
Words	4	1	10	6
Incorrection Information:	144	51	76	45
Proper Names	40	14	27	16
Words	24	8	24	14
Codes and Delimiters	31	11	17	10
Punctuation	13	5	3	2
Format	15	5	3	2
Capitalization	8	3	—	—
Spaces	6	2	—	—
Numeric	5	2	2	1
Diacritics	2	1	—	—
Totals	283	100	168	99

available to us for this study. Table 11 shows the actual errors found by category. In the first category, we note the errors that were detected by the sequence check used by both institutions. These errors could be assigned to any of several causes but because their frequency of occurrence is significant and the checking procedures are so obvious, it seems better to consider this as a separate global category that would be standard procedure in almost any installation. We note that the proportion of sequence errors in the Stanford sample (40/287) is higher than in the Harvard sample (9/168), and this can presumably be attributed to two basic causes. First, the Stanford sample had more cards per entry; hence, a higher likelihood that the cards within an entry would be scrambled. Second, in the Stanford sample an identification number was keyboarded by the operator and any error in this keyboarding operating would be detected by the sequence check.

The next category of errors (including those detected by the input program and those detected later by human proofreading operations) are those due to missing information. In each case the largest single subcategory was the group that we have classified as "missing codes and delimiters." Here the ratios are about the same for each source, and it would appear that although these errors are easy to detect, there is nonetheless a certain basic error-rate that must be accepted in this direction.

The next most popular subcategory of errors in the Stanford sample was "missing spaces," of which 23 appeared in the Stanford sample and none in the Harvard sample (although our own analysis shows that there was at least one of these that was not caught by the human proofreading operation). This sharp distinction between the two situations points out the problem, mentioned previously, of training operators and then checking them during the training period. Almost all of the missing space errors in the Stanford sample occurred at about position 72 in the first line of the record. One is thus naturally led to the conclusion that Stanford was following a convention of keyboarding only in the first 72 columns of the card and that one or more of the operators, at least during the period on which this study was based, had some difficulty in coping with the convention. That this is a local error and one that is correctable is shown by the fact that it tended to occur in clumps within the Stanford sample and was almost nonexistent in the Harvard sample. (It is also possible, though we have not checked this point, that in the Harvard sample a somewhat simpler end of card space convention was used.)

Having noted this particular anomaly in the Stanford sample, we further note that the second most popular Harvard sample error in this general category was "missing capitalization" in codes. These occurred almost entirely in the rendering of the titles of documents and again tended to occur in clumps in the Harvard sample. This suggests that one or more of the Harvard operators had some difficulty understanding the capitalization requirements for their production of titles, and while this presumably was corrected later when noticed by the proofreader, it demonstrates once again the utility of having the easy-to-program error checks built in even though their yield might vary widely from one sample to another.

Apart from the above-mentioned categories, we see that the ratio of sub-categories to the total number of errors is approximately the same for the two samples. Some of these missing entries or missing pieces of information could be detected by machine rules and others could not, but we will return to this issue later.

The third major category of Table 11 lists those errors that occur due to incorrect information that was provided. In this part of the table we see that in both samples the most popular form of error was in rendering proper names, and the ratio of the two checks fairly well with the over-all error ratio. Here, of course, there are rather severe problems in automatic error-detection because of the peculiarity of the spelling rules for proper-name entries, abbreviations that are allowed in various transliteration schemes from non-Roman alphabets, and so forth.

Within this category, the second most popular error for the Stanford sample and the third most popular error for the Harvard sample had to do with incorrect renderings of codes and delimiters. Here the Stanford rate seems to be a bit higher than the Harvard rate but this is most likely a reflection of the larger proportion of the Stanford records that are devoted to the use of codes and delimiters.

The third most important subcategory in the incorrect renderings for Stanford was "misspelled words"; this entry ran second in the Harvard list. In each case 24 errors were observed. Here the relatively high rate in the Harvard sample undoubtedly is related to the much higher proportion of foreign titles in their sample and many of the errors are due to misspellings in non-English words. Of the remaining errors of format (capitalizations, spacing, and so forth), Stanford tends to run higher than Harvard, but that would be expected with their more complicated over-all format.

4.5. The Problem of Automatic Detection

With the above information as a data base, we are in a position to investigate various possible schemes for automatic error-detection. We have already noted that any simple rules that can be programmed effectively probably should be programmed on the grounds that they will provide protection against large numbers of naive errors produced by newly trained operators. In this category we now place the sequence errors, the incorrect or invalid codes and incorrect formats, and the missing codes, spaces, and capitals. The first part of Table 12 notes all of the errors actually detected by the automatic checks used at the two institutions together with those errors that would have been detected by other elementary checks. This accounts for 127 errors in the Stanford sample and 85 errors in the Harvard sample, which corresponds to 44.3 percent of the errors actually found in the former and 51.2 percent of the errors found in the latter.

The question now arises as to what routines would be practical and economical to add to these obvious and simple program routines to obtain a higher proportion of the errors actually found. Let us consider these in the order of the over-all importance in terms of the proportion of the errors not detected by the simple routines.

Proper Names

An examination of the proper names (Table 13) shows that it would be very difficult to set up an algorithm that would be of sufficient sophistication to catch errors of the kind that actually occur. In the Stanford sample, however, the author's name appears frequently in two positions—in

Table 12   Analysis of Potential Error-Detection Possibilities

First Level (including those actually detected by machine in operation):

	Stanford	Harvard
Sequence	40	9
Codes and Delimiters	52	47
Spaces	23	–
Capitalization	8	26
Format	4	3
	127	85

Second Level:

Proper Names	8	–
Words	7	7
Capitalization	8	–
Space	6	–
Numeric	5	2
	34	9
Total Machine-Detectable:	161	94

Table 13   Misspelled Proper Names

Stanford		Harvard	
Incorrect Form	Correct Form	Incorrect Form	Correct Form
Mortig	Moritz	la timore	Lattimore
Cristol	Crisol	Liantung	Liaotung
Luid	Luis	Walther	Walter
Herman	Hermann (4)	ananking	Nanking
Dostojewaski	Dostojewski	Hs	Hsu
Jean de me	Jijena	Mippon	Nippon
Valvuena	Valbuena	Lylton	Lytton (4)
Esponosa	Espinosa	Mancurian	Manchurian
Flexman	Flaxman	Mandhcourie	Mandchourie
Japanes	Japanese	Mower	Moore
Kenneth	Thomas (*sic*)	Modehammer	Modlhammer
Mohammadon	Islam (*sic*)	Pernkoff	Pernikoff (2)
Westminister	Westminster	Manchurei	Mandschurei
Spainish	Spanish	Fomidheva	Fomicheva
Meyers	Myers	Vestric	Vestnik
Strippes	Stippes	Tairen	Dairen
Rugolfus	Rudolfus	Cri'uan-crun	Ch'uan-tsziun
Whit	White	Chlin, T'ung-chih	Rudakov, A
Weinraub	Weintraub	Knoepfnacher	Knoepfmacher
Bak	Bark	Moskva	Leningrad
His	Hippocrates	Anggio	Cinggis
Connelly	Donnelly	Ubymzhiev	Ultnzhiev
Hsiteler	Heitler	Uam-Ude	Ulan-Ude
Raleigh	Rayleigh		
Christian	Christiaan		
Williams	William		
Guthrice	Guthrie		
Janius	Junius		
Inston	Winston		
PrinticHall	Prentice-Hall		
MacMillian	Macmillan		
Frederikc	Frederick		

one case as a specific entry entitled "author," in another case after the letters "by." Thus there is a built-in redundancy that could be used to detect some of the errors. An examination of the errors actually made shows that only 8 of the 40 errors made in the Stanford sample could have been so detected; of course none of the proper-name errors in the Harvard sample could have been detected by this means because this kind of redundancy was not present.

Misspelled Words

Trained keyboard operators rarely make mistakes that can be caught by simple algorithms in the machine. (At least they rarely make such mistakes and fail to correct them on the spot.) In the samples given here we do find a number of errors that could be caught either because the entry did not contain a vowel or because it had illegitimate or highly unlikely sequences of letters (Table 14). In both the Stanford and Harvard samples it appears that about seven of the errors made in each could be so detected.

Capitalization and Other Errors

In the capitalization errors—that is, words that were incorrectly capitalized—there were eight errors that could be detected in the Stanford sample because they involved capitalization of the word "see" and this violated the capitalization conventions. In addition, more sophisticated space-checking and number-checking routines would enable us to catch 11 more errors in the Stanford sample and 2 more errors in the Harvard sample. If these more sophisticated routines were to be incorporated, the total number of errors caught by automatic means would have been increased by 34 additional errors in the Stanford sample and 9 additional errors in the Harvard sample. At this point the proportion of actual errors potentially detected by all procedures is 56.1 percent for the Stanford sample and 56.5 percent for the Harvard sample.

It is clear that most of the remaining errors could only be detected by reference to some kind of an authority list. A missing diacritic in a proper name, the spelling of a proper name, failure to copy the proper punctuation, a missing comma in a title, and so forth, are items that would be very difficult to detect by any but the most sophisticated error-checking routines or by reference to an authority list of considerable proportions. The use of an authority list may have some utility for subject headings (for which there is already some indication of the trading of authority lists in machine-readable form from one library to another). If Stanford had used a standard authority list, some of the spelling errors made in the rendering of subject headings could have been checked against this list. However, it is well to recognize that the difficulty in constructing an authority list is comparable to the difficulty in keyboarding the bibliographic records themselves, and one is therefore not really solving the problem but only transferring it from one area to another area of the over-all operation.

4.6. Detection of Errors Through Subsequent Usage

While the determination of authority lists for the various fields of the bibliographic records may be difficult before the fact, the listing of the

Table 14   Misspelled Words

Stanford		Harvard	
Incorrect Forms	Correct Forms	Incorrect Forms	Correct Forms
paging	pagings	southern	south
bt	by (2)	sociaty	society
publishihg	publishing	secretaria	secretariat
strenght	strength	leagueo	league
su5day	sunday	education	educational
y2y	by	institute	institutions
6ibrary	library	pridiques	juridique
sustems	systems	juges	jugese
freedon	freedom	arean	arena
slaveowners	slave-owners	sotsialist	sotsialisticheskoe
unknowm	unknown	severno vast	severo-vostochnom
antiquites	antiquities	demskrati	demokrati
rhe	the	peopl-e	people
den	der	to-p-o-gr-aphie	topographische
medieaval	medieval	monpolee	mongolie
catchresses	catachrese	kaisiereich	kaiserreich
ith	with	gizinskoi	girinskoi
agricultrure	agriculture	pzovintsii	provintsii
uellow	yellow	pabot	rabot
by	von	sotsizlizu	sotsializm
s e	see	in-t	institute
Merwurdige	Merkwürdige	vostoko-veseniia	narodov azii
Prolog	Prologo		

words or sequences of characters that occur in each field after the fact can be very useful from the error-checking point of view and from other points of view as well. If we assume that the automatic error-checking capability is of the order of the figures given here, namely between 50 and 60 percent, then we can consider how one is to get the remaining errors out of the system. At both Stanford and Harvard the transcribed data was completely proofread. This, of course, does not eliminate all errors, but it does enable one to greatly reduce the number of residual errors in the system. However, it is clear that the bibliographic records will be used for a variety of reasons and that there should be a means of detecting and correcting the small residue of errors even after a proofreading operation. The form that this takes will be determined to a large degree by the needs of the individual library and the uses to which it puts its catalog. A few examples should indicate the possibilities. For instance, there is already some indication that libraries are willing to trade copies of their machine-readable subject authority lists and it is a relatively simple problem to set up comparator programs that would enable one to find all of those entries on one list that were not on the other. If the two lists are largely comparable, then this should lead to the detection of certain errors. Whether such a comparison would be economically justifiable on the grounds of detecting errors alone is questionable. However, the utility of knowing what subject coverage is unique to a given library and what subject coverage is available from another library is probably of sufficient value to the librarians as well as to the users of the library to make this a worthwhile operation.

4.7. Conclusion

We conclude that it is both technically very difficult and economically very unattractive to detect all or almost all of the catalog card conversion errors by automatic procedures. Rather, one should program all of the simple procedures that are appropriate to the particular bibliographic record to allow for quick error-checking of the output of newly trained keyboard operators, and then augment this with more sophisticated routines to the extent that increased programming and run costs are balanced by the increased yield of errors.

The fact that 90 or 95 percent error-detection does not appear feasible means that there is a heavier burden placed on the initial quality control operation and on the proofreading operation than would otherwise be necessary. Clearly, the most important phase is the quality control operation where formal records should be kept of the procedures used, the errors detected, and the kinds of errors made by the various operators. Following good quality control procedures, feedback should go directly to the operators themselves and should be accomplished on a timely basis— that is, in sufficient time for them to correct any high-frequency errors they are making before too many of these errors get into the system. Finally, a continuing error-correction capability should be maintained and merged with the use of the catalog listing for other purposes. This will eventually tend to clean up the large proportion of residual errors as a by-product of other necessary and useful operations.

References

1. Cox and Dolby, "Structured Linguistic Data and the Automatic Detection of Errors," *Advances in Computer Typesetting*, Institute of Printing, London, 1966.
2. Cox, Dews, and Dolby, *The Computer and the Library*, Archon Press, Hamden, Connecticut, 1967.

3. De Gennaro, Richard, "A Computer-Produced Shelf List," *Coll. Res. Libr.* 26 (1965) 311-315/353.
4. Johnson, Richard D., "A Book Catalog at Stanford," *J. Library Automation*, 1 (1968) 13-50.
5. *Programmer's Guide, PL/1 (F)*, IBM Systems Reference Library, 1966.

PART II: UTILITY

5 The Structure of the Shelf List of the Fondren Library at Rice University

5.1. Introduction

Many of the questions concerning library automation, particularly those centered about the utility of machine-readable library catalogs, can only be studied by a thorough-going investigation of the content and structure of existing card catalogs. In general, an exhaustive study of any aspect of the card catalog is too costly, and it is necessary to resort to the study of restricted samples which, to the desired extent, reflect the properties of the complete card catalog. For most purposes, a *random sample* is the most useful kind, but unfortunately it is difficult and expensive to select one from the usual library card catalogs.

One of the potential advantages of automated library catalogs is that the selection of random samples, as well as completely detailed studies of information contained in the catalog and of the organization of its information can be performed at low cost levels and with very rapid "turn-around times."[1]

As we shall show below, the information contained in the catalog, together with a low cost and rapid means of retrieving it (such as a computerized catalog would provide), can turn the catalog into a powerful tool for the administration and management of the library.

This chapter describes a random sample drawn from the shelf list of the Fondren Library at Rice University, Houston, Texas. Approved statistical procedures were used for all of the components of the selection technique to ensure reliability of the sample. No purpose would be served to recount the details here; more important for us are the properties of the sample.

---

[1]"Turn-around time" is a term used by computermen for the elapsed time between submission of a task to a computation center and its completion. Thus turn-around time includes not only that actual time required by the computing machines but also handling time, waiting time in the queue, and possibly even the time needed to program the task. This term seems well-adapted to library processes.

The Random Sample was drawn from the shelf list rather than from the main public catalog to minimize user inconvenience. Moreover, the almost one-to-one correspondence of the shelf list with the items constituting the physical collection increases the accuracy with which a small random sample can reflect the entire collection. This means, for instance, that the duplication of monograph references provided by the Subject and Title cards in the Subject-Title catalog is avoided.[2] Finally, in a phase of this project not yet begun, it is hoped to obtain an estimate of the rate of "loss" of cards in the public catalog (due to misfiling, unauthorized card removal, and all other causes). It is generally recognized that there is some loss, but we have been unable to locate any statistics concerned with this question that would enable one to estimate the impact on users and the cost of maintaining a public card catalog at a given level of completeness. These questions are closely related to the problem of justifying the cost of book catalogs. In any event, selection of the Sample from the shelf list, which is open only to the library's professional staff, provides a means for estimating the loss rate in the public catalog. The size of the Sample selected, about 1900 cards, was determined so as to enable one to detect public catalog losses of economically significant dimensions.

It is usually difficult to get a reliable estimate of the number of items stored in a given library collection. This is due in part to the ever-increasing growth rates experienced by most modern libraries and a consequent swamping of their cataloging operations. The Fondren estimates that there were as of Spring 1968 perhaps 40,000 uncatalogued items which do not appear in any way in the shelf list.[3] Moreover, were all items represented in the shelf list, there would be no universally accepted means for counting them. Certain items require more than one shelf list card (because of information run-over), which cards can correspond to only one physical item. Other (single) cards correspond to numerous physical volumes, e.g., many "Collected Works." In this paper we will try to estimate the statistical distributions of the number of volumes per card, and the number of cards per title, to enable one to estimate whichever of these variables one desires from the raw count of the number of cards in the sample, and the ratio of the size of the sample to the size of the card collection.

5.2. Shelf List Statistics

The shelf list at Fondren contains a single title card for each serial publication acquired by the library. A separate catalog, which was not

[2]The Fondren Library public catalog is an Author-Title-Subject file, which would still further dilute the utility of a random sample of given size.

[3]Reference 1, p. 44. This backlog presumably does not contain periodicals.

sampled, contains information about the receipt of individual issues and numbers of the serial. Hence, a count of the proportion of cards in the Random Sample that refer to serial publications provides an estimate of the number of serials in the total collection (which will be given below). However, the Sample can neither provide any information about the average number of physical volumes per serial title in the collection, nor can it provide other statistics that would easily be obtained from a study of the separate serials shelf list.

Collection Size

The Fondren Sample consists of 1926 catalog cards. The distribution of the number of cards per catalog drawer is given in Figure 13. From this information it follows that there are about 267,743 cards in the Fondren shelf list, with 826 being the average number of cards per catalog drawer. This means that 0.0072, or about 3/4 percent, of the shelf list is contained in the Random Sample. As will appear in the sequel, even so small a sample is already representative of many properties of the total collection.

The distribution shown in Figure 13 is closely fit by the normal probability distribution ("bell-shaped curve") of statistics, as is readily seen by graphing the data points on (cumulative) probability scale graph paper. Figure 14 displays such a graph. Inspection shows that the standard deviation of the distribution is about 135 cards. To the extent that the mean and standard deviation for tray contents as observed at Fondren are typical for libraries using trays of the same size, this information can be used to predict the total number of catalog trays that will be needed to house a card catalog collection of any given size.

Collection Breakdown

Of the 1926 cards in the Sample, 60 of them had some designation explicitly indicating that the collection subset to which it referred was a serial publication. Thus, since 3.11 percent of the Sample were so designated, there must be about 8330 serials so designated in the entire shelf list.

We recognized eight of the sample cards as referring to serial publications, although there was no explicit designation to indicate that further information about these items would be found in the serials shelf list. In general, these items appear to belong to periodicals that ceased publication before the Fondren Library was founded at the beginning of this century, but we have not introduced a formal process that would distinguish them. The estimated proportion of such serials not so designated is $8/1926 = 0.415$ percent, which adds 1111 serials not so designated to the collection.

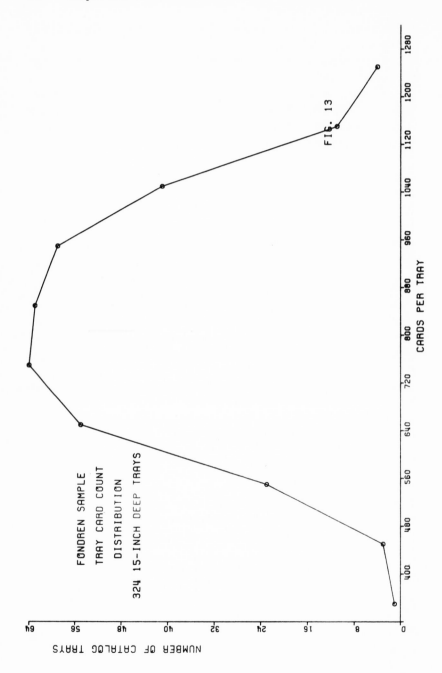

FONDREN SAMPLE
TRAY CARD COUNT
DISTRIBUTION
324 15-INCH DEEP TRAYS

FIG. 13

CARDS PER TRAY

NUMBER OF CATALOG TRAYS

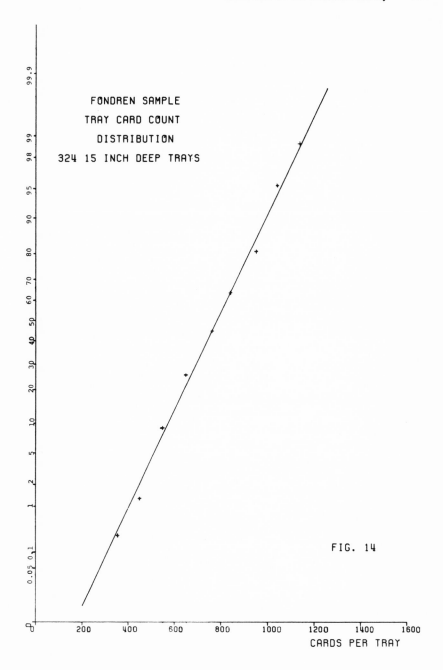

FONDREN SAMPLE
TRAY CARD COUNT
DISTRIBUTION
324 15 INCH DEEP TRAYS

FIG. 14

CARDS PER TRAY

The total number of serials in the collection is thus estimated to be 9441.

It appears that shelf-list cards were handwritten during the early years of the Fondren collection, and although most of these have long since been replaced by typewritten or printed cards there still remain a few of the originals. There were 15 in the Sample, which is 0.0078 of it. This means that approximately 2090 handwritten cards still remain in the complete shelf list. These handwritten cards are all deficient in bibliographical information, so any attempt to find and convert all of them to typed or printed form will require that a certain (frequently substantial) amount of cataloging effort be undertaken. If we conservatively assume that locating and modernizing one handwritten card will cost $10, then more than $20,000 will be needed to update the complete shelf list. This is one of the irreducible costs that would have to be considered in any estimate of the cost of converting the Fondren shelflist to machine-readable form. It most likely applies also to many other university libraries founded before or during the early years of typewriting machines.

Since cataloging costs are growing along with and at least at the same exponential rate as acquisitions (see below for details), while competent cataloging personnel are becoming increasingly more difficult to find, it is of some importance to determine the saving in human handling due to Library of Congress (LC) printed catalog cards. In principle, once an acquisition has been bibliographically identified, it can be determined whether LC provides a catalog card for it. However, LC will not usually provide cards for editions later than the first or for republication of items (sometimes differing in minor ways from the original). In these cases the LC card must be amended, usually by the "strike-out and type over" technique. Of course, if the LC card data were in machine-readable form, this last process could be performed using a remote terminal with a display screen, so as to produce uniform, clean copy output cards with a slightly reduced human effort.

For our examination of the Fondren Random Sample we have agreed to call a catalog card an "LC card" if the card exhibits some explicit identification of LC origin. This usually takes the form of a printed notation in the lower left corner of the card. Our definition underestimates the true number of LC cards in the sample, first because only the last in a sequence of continuation cards will normally contain the identifying indicator, and second because we do not know if all cards produced by LC have an identifying indicator. Both of these phenomena are minor perturbations which are not of great significance.

Of the 1926 cards in the Sample, 1275 (66 percent) were LC cards that had not required changing; another 68 (3.5 percent) were changed LC cards. There were 472 (24.5 percent) typed, nonserial cards in the Sample.

The significant conclusion that can be extracted from the above is that even if catalog cards were available from LC for some edition of each acquired monograph, the ratio 68/1275 is likely to represent, at least in first approximation, the proportion of LC cards that will require local modification. This means that 5.3 percent of the acquisitions processed will require card data modification by the cataloging staff. We stress here that serials have been excluded from these considerations, and it should also be pointed out that the backlog of uncataloged material at Fondren, and elsewhere, will often consist of items for which LC cards are not likely to be available.

Corporate Authorship

The distinction between personal authorship and corporate authorship of monographs and documents is one of the properties used in information retrieval systems. Different document identification procedures must be used, and the techniques used to correct or at least to recognize incorrect or incomplete retrieval requests will be dependent on the class to which the item to be retrieved belongs. Since one of the proposed virtues of automated library catalogs is their utility and versatility in the retrieval process—which is, after all, simply an extension of the role the card catalog now plays—it will be useful to know how the monograph collection is partitioned between the two classes of authors.

We will say that an author is a *personal author* if the first line on the catalog card (other than those lines displaying the call number) exhibits a personal name with or without titles (such as *Sir, Pres., Lord,* etc.) and, optionally, birth and/or death dates, but nothing else. If any further indicator is given, or if the first line does not contain a personal name, and if the card does not refer to a serial, then the card is said to be *corporately authored.* Corporate authorship, according to this definition, includes unauthored, nonserial items, as well as items represented by cards displaying a personal name followed, for instance, by one of the following: *ed., comp., trans., defendent,* etc.

With these conventions, 13 percent of the nonserial cards were corporately authored, and approximately one in ten of the corporately authored items is a map. Table 15 summarizes the statistics discussed thus far.

Language Distribution

The Sample contains 1830 cards that refer to textual works other than serials. Included in the residue of 28 nontextual, nonserial items are maps,

Table 15   Summary of Statistics

		Percent
LC cards	1275	66.2
Modified LC cards	68	3.5
Typed nonserial	472	24.5
Handwritten	15	0.8
Designated serial	60	3.1
Nondesignated serial	8	0.4
Subtotal	1898	98.5
Maps, music, etc.	28	1.5
Total	1926	100.0

Table 16   Distribution of Textual Non-Serial Cards vs. Language of Work

Language	Number in Sample	Percent of 1829
English	1355	74.08
German	215	11.76
French	146	7.98
Italian	38	2.78
Spanish	33	1.81
Latin	13	0.71
Portuguese	13	0.71
Russian	7	0.38
Icelandic	3	0.16
Polish	2	0.11
Swedish	2	0.11
Dutch	1	0.05
Japanese	1	0.05

folios of drawings, and musical scores, all of which are represented in the shelf list. Table 16 displays the distribution of nonserial textual works according to the "language of the work," defined as the language of the title of the item as shown on the shelf list card. The significance of this language distribution is discussed in Chapter 6. The high proportion of English occurring in the Sample is not typical of all libraries; the Library of Congress has had, for the past twenty years at least, only 50 percent of its nonoriental monograph acquisitions in English, while the Stanford University Undergraduate Catalog reveals, as one would expect, only a trivial number of non-English volumes (less than five percent).

Volumes Per Title

Figure 15 displays the frequency-ranked proportion of the Sample as a function of the number of physical volumes per card for nonserials. This distribution decreases less rapidly than the exponential. If a random sample of N nonserial cards is drawn from the Fondren shelf list, then one can expect to find approximately

$$(0.905 + 0.109 + 0.043 + 0.026 + 0.020 +$$
$$0.027 + 0.019 + 0.014 + 0.010)N$$

physical volumes on the shelf. That is, $(1.173)N$ volumes for N nonserial shelf list cards randomly chosen. It is likely that this expansion ratio is applicable to most university and archival collections, but we have not been able to verify this point.

Fewer than 1 percent of the cards in the Sample are not the first card in a sequence of cards with a given class number. Of those that are second or third cards, the greatest single subset is accounted for by the map classification category.

Book Length

How verbose are authors? How long is a book? We have examined the distribution of the monographs in the Sample as a function of the number of pages they contain and displayed the results in Figure 16. For this purpose we defined the number of pages in a book to be the Arabic number indicated on the catalog card in initial position (or following the Roman pagination indication if one exists) in the pagination portion of the catalog entry. Thus bibliographical pages explicitly indicated in the catalog entry were not counted (but see Chapter 7). The class of items called "pamphlets," and frequently defined as items consisting of fewer than 49 pages, does not appear to be distinguished in a significant way by the distribution. This suggests that the partition of the collection into pamphlet and nonpamphlet items is artificial. The mean number of pages in a monograph is 276.6. The distribution will be of some utility in projecting the amount of storage space required to store the *contents* of books in machine-readable form, although other factors, including the distribution of the number of characters per page must also be considered.

5.3. Exponential Growth of Collections

It is a matter of great practical importance to know the rate of growth of a library collection, for upon this information is based most future planning concerned with physical plant expansion, personnel requirements, and future funding needs. It is not often realized that the current growth rate and the growth rates of the recent past (i.e., the previous 10 to 20 years) do not suffice for a valid estimate of future growth, but this information, together with similar information for short time intervals

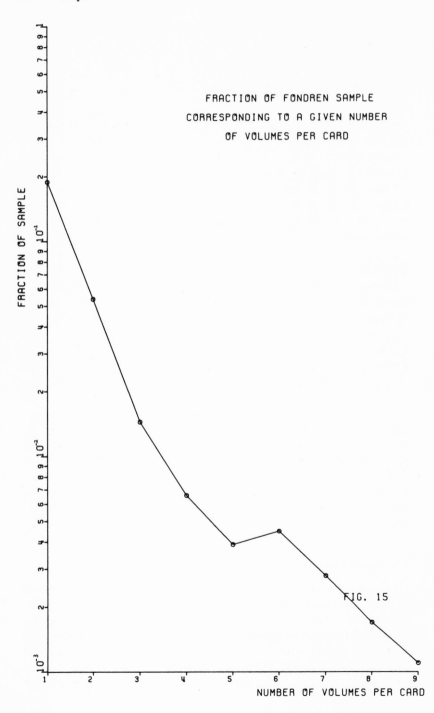

FRACTION OF FONDREN SAMPLE
CORRESPONDING TO A GIVEN NUMBER
OF VOLUMES PER CARD

FIG. 15

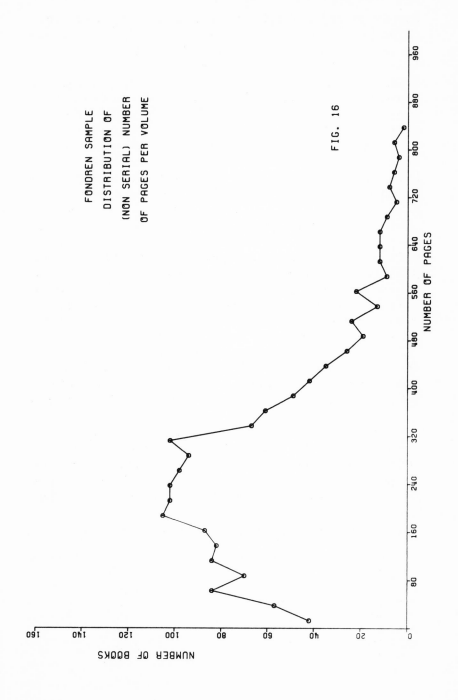

FONDREN SAMPLE
DISTRIBUTION OF
(NON SERIAL) NUMBER
OF PAGES PER VOLUME

FIG. 16

spanning the previous *centuries,* clarifies the dynamic processes that affect collection growth and makes more reliable estimation possible. The same information has much to tell us about the growth and state of civilization, but this vast theme can but be touched upon here.

Figure 17 displays the number of Sample items as a function of century of imprint date. In Table 17 the annual growth rate and the number of years required for the collection to double *(doubling period)* is shown for data from Figure 17.

That part of the Sample with imprint date in the 1960's has been omitted from the calculations in Table 17 because of the perturbing effect of the time interval that elapses between the publication of an item and its acquisition and cataloging by the library. Also, the numbers for the sixteenth century and seventeenth century are too small to be reliable.

Table 17 indicates that the maximum rate of growth of the collection (by imprint date) is less than 2.5 percent. Since the general rate of growth of the United States economy, as measured by the Gross National Product (GNP) estimator, has been more than 4 percent, it would seem that the much-heralded library "explosion" will not have any serious consequences, as the current rate (and even an increased rate) of growth of investment in libraries *could* be maintained by the economy, *if* the accessions growth rate is not too different from the imprint growth rate.

Questions pertaining to administrative or political issues, or to the possibility of increasing private endowment funds to keep pace with the national economic growth, have not been considered in this conclusion, and will of course have a major effect on the ability of individual libraries to respond to the growth challenge.

We appear to have concluded that the library "explosion" is only a reality in the sense that library holdings increase as an exponential function of imprint date, but that it ought to have little effect on libraries or the way in which they are run, because the growth rate is comfortably less than that of the economy and can therefore be managed by an increasingly

Table 17   Doubling Period and Annual Growth Rate by Centuries

Centuries	Doubling Period, years	Annual Growth Rate, percent
16th-17th	63.09	1.10
17th-18th	32.39	2.16
18th-19th	60.62	1.15
19th-1949	33.89	2.07
1949-1959	28.75	2.44

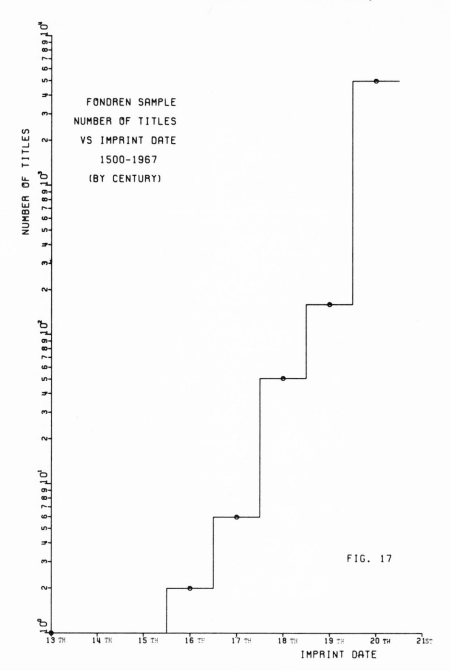

FONDREN SAMPLE
NUMBER OF TITLES
VS IMPRINT DATE
1500-1967
(BY CENTURY)

NUMBER OF TITLES

IMPRINT DATE

FIG. 17

extensive application of current technique, methods of administration, and funds. But these conclusions follow from a superficial view of growth during long time intervals, intervals much longer than those with which the planner or administrator is or can be effectively concerned. If we turn to the other extreme, and only consider library growth during the interval of the very recent past, then the situation is different. For example, the Fondren Sample shows that growth for the 20 years 1940-59 was at an annual rate of 6.64 percent with a doubling period of 10.79 years. This interval includes the years of United States involvement in World War II, which should, one would expect, depress the growth rate for the initial segment of the two-decade period, and thus inflate the estimated growth rate for that 20-year interval. Nevertheless, we must conclude that *for this period* the rate of growth of the Fondren Library collection was much closer to the rate of growth of the Gross National Product. Other comparable libraries probably exhibit a similar pattern of growth. These two sets of extreme growth rate estimates—the one extending over several centuries, the other over a decade or two—each provide partial views of the growth phenomenon which can be reconciled by an examination of the entire Sample by decade of imprint as seen in Figure 18. The decade 1820-29 yielded only five items in the Sample; clearly this and all preceding decades supply too little information for us to be able to discriminate any short-term trends.[1] Excluding pre-1820-29 data, it is apparent that the graph is reasonably well fit by a straight line, which (since the graph paper is semilogarithmic) corresponds to exponential growth, as before. But it is also clear that there are two significant departures from linearity, one occurring in passage from the 1860 decade to the 1870's, and the other from the 1930's through and including the 1940's. In the former case the absolute number of acquisitions actually declined; in the latter it grew slowly during the thirties above the figure for the previous decade and remained nearly constant for the next decade. The numbers occurring for the 1840 decade to 1850 decade shrinkage are small, and their difference is only 1, so we will not consider that transition.

This suggests that a better approximation to the observations will be obtained by fitting three straight lines to the data, for the periods 1840 to 1869, 1870 to 1929, and 1940 to 1959. (Post-1959 data is excluded for the reason given earlier in this section.) The lines were fit to the data using the usual least squares criterion. Table 18 exhibits the doubling period and annual growth rate corresponding to each of the fitting lines.

---

[1]This incidentally illustrates the necessity for the facility to obtain random shelf list samples of a larger size in a rapid and inexpensive manner. The current sample is large enough to focus attention on the phenomenon but too small to delineate it.

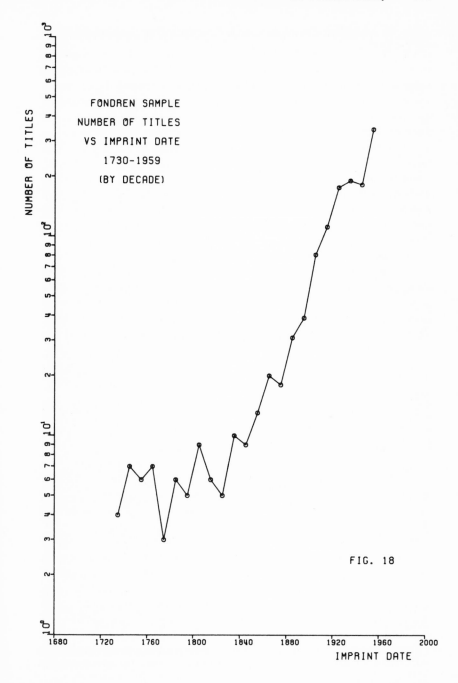

FONDREN SAMPLE
NUMBER OF TITLES
VS IMPRINT DATE
1730-1959
(BY DECADE)

NUMBER OF TITLES

IMPRINT DATE

FIG. 18

Table 18 Doubling Period and Annual Growth Rate Corresponding to Fitting Lines

Interval	Doubling Period, years	Annual Growth Rate, percent
1840 to 1869	17.36	4.02
1870 to 1929	15.17	4.66
1940 to 1959	10.79	6.64

Unfortunately the third time interval supplies only two points, which determine a straight line. Were the Sample considerably larger than it is, it would have been possible to estimate the lines using annual data, and thus have at least twenty data points per line. This will have to await some future study.

The first two lines have nearly the same slope, and hence correspond to approximately equal growth rates. The last line, associated with the most recent period for which data are available, appears to imply a significantly more rapid rate of growth. However, in this instance the absolute number of items per year appearing in the sample is large enough to enable us to calculate a fitting line for the 1950 to 59 period based on annual data. The resultant annual growth rate and doubling period estimates for the data for the 1950's alone are 3.54 percent and 19.90 years, respectively; the decade of the fifties was relatively slow in growth compared with the two-decade period 1940 to 59.

The significant differences in doubling period (and hence annual growth) that occur when different time intervals are chosen for the calculations makes it imperative that more serious study be devoted to this question. Plant and personnel requirements and the ability to predict them are based upon this statistic. The lack of stability of growth rates associated with nonstationary time series such as GNP, or holdings as a function of imprint date, has long been known. Reference 2 contains an elaborate discussion of this problem.

The foregoing growth estimates have all been concerned with collection growth as a function of date of imprint of the acquired items rather than date of accession. Now observe that the yearly accessions of any library will inevitably include items which have imprints covering a span of years, and hence estimation of collection growth by means of imprint date must underestimate the actual amount of accessions growth. This could be quite a considerable underestimation. Suppose, for instance, that $1/2^{n+1}$ of annual accessions have imprint dates n years prior to the accession year. Then one-half of current accessions will bear the imprint of the current year, one-quarter that of the previous year, and so forth.

How fast can libraries grow? And for how long? Certainly, as we have already argued above, they cannot sustain growth more rapid than the growth in gross national product. The imprint date growth estimates show that the growth rate of accessions is at least exponential, and, for the Fondren Library, annual imprint growth is less than annual GNP growth; but these two growth rates are not very different.

The significant conclusion that must be drawn is that the distribution of acquisitions by imprint date provides an absolute lower bound for the actual annual accession distribution. It is the latter that is directly correlated with the budget, and hence must be understood in some detail. It is likely that there is a natural imprint date distribution of annual accessions, and it is also probable that this distribution follows the geometric decrease illustrated by the fictional "$1/2^{n+1}$ law" above. Data normally available in most libraries do not include the necessary information to answer this question. It should certainly be obtained in a future study.

We will make the formal hypothesis that the stationary growth rate of library holdings by accession year is approximately equal to the growth rate of the United States Gross National Product. A detailed discussion of the data on which the hypothesis is grounded is given in Chapter 6 of this volume. It therefore remains to examine the nonstationary intervals of library growth, which simply means that the departures from approximate linearity shown in Figure 18 must be investigated. Their most striking common feature is that they both occur during historical periods of great social dislocation; we observe that the 1930's and 1940's saw economic disintegration, the rise to significant power of two new social ideologies, a global war, and large-scale refugee movements. The 1870's saw the sudden reduction of the literate population and the economic and political disintegration of the Southern states in the United States, and the Franco-Prussian War. We do not mean to suggest that war is the primary cause of nonstationarity of the acquisition by imprint date statistic—the periods encompassing the U.S. Civil War and the First World War are uninfluenced by the conflicts. Rather, we believe that the falling off of the acquisition's growth is a measure related to social dislocation and change. The data are too sparse for us to claim them as evidence for this view; they have merely suggested an intriguing possibility which more extensive study of the *structure* of library collections (as opposed to the content of the items constituting the collection) will in time answer.

From a more immediately utilitarian viewpoint, a librarian planning in 1945 for the construction of a facility to house his growing collection throughout one doubling period would in 1955 be very surprised had he in 1945 used his acquisition growth rate for the previous few years. His projected growth and doubling period would likely have been about 2 percent and 33 years, or less. A retrospective view in 1955 (with 23 years left to go to complete the projected doubling period) would show an actual growth rate of more than 6 percent and a doubling period of 10.8 years, which he would readily recognize since his ten-year-old facility would be full. This simply illustrates the importance of being able to recognize the "normal" growth periods and to distinguish their statistics from those of the transient periods. In turn, this requires a continuing process of maintaining and updating statistical information about individual collections, and a smaller but serious research effort to determine the nature of the holdings acquired in the past. Expressed in other words, the relationship between accession distributions and imprint distributions should be carefully studied, and statistics should be regularly maintained and updated.

5.4. Analysis by Class Number

The Library of Congress classification system, which has always been used by the Fondren, attempts to classify the areas of human knowledge in a manner that permits of progressive refinement by subdivision. It should therefore be possible to determine the principal areas of human interest at different times in the past by analyzing the distribution of LC categories by imprint date in a library collection. Apart from the general light that this might throw on the history of civilization, it should also indicate those portions of library collections that should be expected to dominate in short term future acquisitions and use.

Table 19 exhibits this distribution for the LC letter class of those cards in the Fondren Sample carrying an imprint date after 1849; the earlier imprints and their class are collected in Table 20. Since the general collection has exponential growth (apart from the nonstationary growth periods), each class category also would have exponential growth if human interests and efforts were uniformly distributed throughout the range of subjects indicated in the LC letter classification. Therefore, to compare the distributions at various times, the relative frequencies for each of the periods rather than the absolute frequencies of occurrence should be used. This simply means that one should estimate the proportion of all items carrying a given imprint date that belong to a given LC letter class. When this is done, it appears, for instance, that the class "E" (History of the United States, non-Local) relative frequency distribution looks as shown in Table 21. The decade of the 1860's is the overwhelming contributor of the "E" class to the collection. It is hard to doubt that we have simply found a "measure" of the relative significance of the American Civil War insofar as

Table 19 Library of Congress Classes vs. Imprint Date (Fondren Sample)

Class	1960's	1950's	1940's	1930's	1920's	1910's	1900's	1890's	1880's	1870's	1860's	1850's
B	7	12	5	4	2	6	1	6	1		1	
BC	2		1	1			1					
BD	3	3	1		1	1	1	1				
BF	4	7	2	4	8	2	2	3				
BJ	2	1			1	2	2					
BL	3	4	2	1	2							
BM			1									
BP						1						
BR	1	2	2	1	1	1						
BS	2	4			1	1						
BT	4	1	1	2	1	1	1					
BV	2	4	1	1	1					1		
BX	7	2	1	3	3				1			
CB		1	1	1	1		1					
CC				1								
CD	1		1									
CJ	1											
CS				3								
CT	2	1	1		1							
D	7	5	11		4	7		1				1
DA	4	1	8	3	3		4	1				
DB		1	1	1			2					1
DC	1	1	1	2	3	2	1	1	1			
DD				1		1	1		1			
DE	2	3		1								

Table 19 (continued)

Class	1960's	1950's	1940's	1930's	1920's	1910's	1900's	1890's	1880's	1870's	1860's	1850's
DF	1	1		2	1		1					
DG	1	1		1	2	2	1					
DH	1											
DK	5	2		2								
DL	1											
DP	2											
DQ						1						
DR		1	3	4	1	2						
DS	12	8	3	2	3							
DT		3	2				1	1				
DU							1				1	
E	12	16	1	3	6	3	7	5	4	2	11	2
F	10	7	6	7	6	5	2	1	1	2		
G	1	1		1								1
GA		1										
GB		1										
GC			1									
GR	1	1				1						
GV	6	1										
GN	1		1			1	1					
H		1										
HB	3	6	3	2					1			
HC	18	5		5	2	2						
HD	15	12	3	2	3	3	1					
HE	2	1										

Table 19 (continued)

Class	1960's	1950's	1940's	1930's	1920's	1910's	1900's	1890's	1880's	1870's	1860's	1850's
HF	3	5		2	1	2	1		1			
HG	8	5		1	4		1				1	
HJ	3	2	2	1								
HM	4	5	1	2	1							
HN	2	3										
HQ	6		1	2		2						
HT		2			1	3	3					
HV	9	1		1	1							
HX	1				1							
JA	3											
JC	5	2	1	2						1		
JF		1								1		
JK	2	1	1	2		2	1					
JN	1	1	1	1								
JQ	1	1										
JS			1		1	1						
JX	1	1	1	1	1	3						
K												
KB	1					3						
KD			1	1			1					
L			1									
LA	3	1		2		1		1				
LB	19	8	3	5	6	1	1					
LC	3	1	2									
LD	1		1	4	1							

Table 19 (continued)

Class	1960's	1950's	1940's	1930's	1920's	1910's	1900's	1890's	1880's	1870's	1860's	1850's
(LT)*	1											
M		2					1					
ML	4	6	4	1	2	2	1	1		1		
MT		1			1	1						
N	3	4	4	1								
NA	3	6	2	2	5	3						
NB	3	1										
NC	1	1										
ND	4	3	1	2	1	1	2					
NK	1		1	1		1		1				
P								1				
PA	6	3	4	5	2	1	1	1				
PC		3	2	1	2				3	2		
PD				1								
PE	3	1	1	2	2	1				1		
PF	3			1	1		1					1
PG	3	1	1		1	2						
PJ		2		2								
PL	1											
PM	1											
PN	6	5	2	9	3	3	2		2			
PQ	21	20	16	8	9	11	11	4	4			
PR	29	16	12	22	23	5	9	3	5	3	1	4
PS	18	15	10	15	10	3	4	3	2	4		2
PT	14	16	9	16	7	6	2	2		1	1	

Table 19 (continued)

Class	1960's	1950's	1940's	1930's	1920's	1910's	1900's	1890's	1880's	1870's	1860's	1850's
Q	3	1	4	1	2	2						
QA	19	7	6	4	2	3	1		2	1	1	
QB	15	5	4	1	1	1	1				1	1
QC	11	1	1	1	1	1	1					
QD	3	3	1	4	3				1			
QE	3	4	1		1		2					
QH	3					3	1					
QK	1				1							
QL	4	7	2	2			1				1	
QP	3	4	2		1							
QR	2			1								
R	1	2	1	1	1							
RA			1	1								
RB		1										
RC	2	1	1			2						
RF		1										
RK		1										
RM			1									
RS		1					1					
S				1								
SB	1	1										
SF		2										
SK		1			2							
T	1	1	1									
TA	4	3	4	2	1							1

Table 19 (continued)

Class	1960's	1950's	1940's	1930's	1920's	1910's	1900's	1890's	1880's	1870's	1860's	1850's
TC			1		1			1				
TD	2	2			1							
TF	2	1			1							
TH	1	1										
TJ	2	2										
TK	1	1	2	3	1							
TL		1										
TN	3	1	2					1				
TP				3								
TR	1			1								
TS			1									
TT	1											
U	3				1	2	1					
UA	4					1	1					
UB			1		1	1						
UC						1						
UD						1						1
V	1		1			1						1
VA			1			1				1		
VC						1						
VM					1							
Z	11	17	6	1	4	1			1			

Table 20   Library of Congress Classes vs. Imprint Date (Fondren Sample)

Integers preceeding LC class indicators show the number of cards belonging to that class.

1840's	B, BD, BX, DC, F, HD, PE, PR, QE, Z.
1830's	DA, DG, HB, HD, JC, PA, 2 PR, QD.
1820's	KA, 2 PA, 2 PR.
1810's	E, F, PQ, 3 PR, DA.
1800's	DA, PN, 2 PQ, 4 PR.
1790's	BC, LB, PR, PS, BJ.
1780's	B, 5 PR.
1770's	F, 2 PR.
1760's	BX, DH, NK, 3 PR.
1750's	DG, ML, PQ, 3 PR.
1740's	B, BJ, DA, PA, 3 PR.
1730's	DA, PN, 2 PR.
1720's	BJ, DF, PS.
1710's	JX, 3 PR.
1700's	DA, PR.
1690's	DA.
1680's	B.
1670's	BX, PQ, QC.
1630's	DR.
1580's	JN.

Table 21   Probability Distribution of the Library of Congress "E" Class from 1850 by Decade

1850	1860	1870	1880	1890	1900
0.154	0.579	0.111	0.129	0.128	0.086

1910	1920	1930	1940	1950	1960
0.027	0.038	0.016	0.005	0.046	0.027

the Fondren, and, perhaps more generally, libraries in the United States are concerned. A check of the 11 shelf list cards in the "E"—1860 decade part of the Sample yielded the following titles:

1864   History of the republic of the United States of America, as traced in the writings of Alexander Hamilton and of his contemporaries.

1864   Southern slavery in its present aspects: containing a reply to a late work of the Bishop of Vermont on slavery.

1865   New York Herald (Issue for April 15, 1865, containing articles on the assassination and death of President Abraham Lincoln).

1861   Providence in war; a Thanksgiving discourse (The Pulpit and rostrum, no. 23).

1864   Shall sympathizers with treason hold seats in Congress? Speech of Hon. Godlove S. Orth, of Ind., on the resolution to expel Mr. Long.

1864   Sufferings endured for a free government; or, A history of the cruelties and atrocities of the rebellion . . .

1867   The lost cause; a new southern history of the war of the Confederates . . . Drawn from official sources . . .

1864   The bivouac and the battlefield; or, Campaign sketches in Virginia and Maryland.

1867   History of the United States secret service.

1865   Life-struggles in Rebel prisons: a record of the sufferings, escapes, adventures and starvation of the Union prisoners.

1864   The philanthropic results of the war in America. Collected from official and other authentic sources, by an American citizen. Dedicated by permission to the United States sanitary commission.

All titles but the first obviously pertain to some aspect or other of the American Civil War. It is attractive to suppose that determination of the distribution of LC classes as a function of time, normalized so that each column (i.e., the LC distribution for a fixed year) sums to 1 will provide a measure, albeit gross, of the relative importance or significance of the various events, discoveries, proposals, and philosophies which compose the fabric of civilization. For instance, the probabilities in Table 21 suggest that the most important "event" in post-1849 United States history was the Civil War and its underlying causes. Moreover, it is likely that much of the 1950's and 1960's "E" class items are centennial appraisals of Civil War events and problems. Once again, a quick check of the Sample answers this question: in each of these two decades, just more than one-third of the items classed "E" in the Sample concern themselves with such issues. This would appear to show that neither the First World War ("E" probability for 1910's = 0.027), the Great Depression ("E" probability for 1930's = 0.016), nor the Second World War ("E" probability for 1940's = 0.005) were nearly as significant historical events as the Civil War. This initially startling conclusion is strengthened when it is recalled that the schism which resulted in the Civil War has not yet healed; that many of the racial problems that we currently face are the shadow of old social systems foundering and their new but inadequate replacements in the epoch of the Civil War.

The sample is small; it cannot display historical phenomena of lesser import with the clarity provided for the "E" class. However, some suggestive results remain to be extracted.

Consideration of class "HG" shows a relative maximum probability of 0.025 for the decade of the 1920's; there is another significant rise from an effectively zero contribution in the 1930's and 1940's to 0.014 in the 1950's, and 0.018 in the 1960's. "HG" is the "Private finance" category of the LC classification scheme. The four titles with 1920's imprint are:

1929   Five men of Frankfort; the story of the Rothschilds.

1926   The amalgamation movement in English banking, 1825-1924.

1925   Principles of corporation finance.

1929   Investments of United States capital in Latin America.

The single "HG" class monograph with 1930's imprint is:

1936   The theory and practice of central banking, with special reference to American experiences, 1913-1935.

Category "HX," "Socialism. Communism. Anarchism.", has the probability distribution shown in Table 22.

The titles are:

1907   Socialism before the French revolution; a history.

1907   From serfdom to socialism (by James Keir Hardie).

1906   Anarchism and socialism (by Georgii Valentinovich Plekhanov).

Table 22   Probability Distribution of the Library of Congress "HX" Class from 1850 by Decade

1850	1860	1870	1880	1890	1900
0.000	0.000	0.000	0.000	0.000	0.037

1910	1920	1930	1940	1950	1960
0.027	0.006	0.000	0.000	0.003	0.002

and

1910   Industrial problems.

1912   My Life (by August Bebel).

1913   The conquest of bread (by Petr Kropotkin).

It is hard for the authors of this paper to avoid the conclusion that the social aspects of "the Communist menace" have not been a matter of serious concern to Americans since the 1920's, and that it most certainly is not one of the major areas of human effort and concern today.

5.5. Conclusions

Properly chosen random samples of library catalogs provide a number of opportunities to study the structure of the catalog as well as the nature of the library's contents. To some extent, the utility of a random sample decreases as full catalogs in machine-readable form come into being: the computer can be used to obtain counts and summaries of the entire set of information rather than from just a sample. However, even with information in machine-readable form it is necessary to program the machine to obtain the required summary, a task that is always time-consuming and, in cases requiring sophisticated interpretation of implicit information may be all but impossible.

However, it is a fairly simple chore to add random numbers to the catalog records in an automated catalog system and then to sort the catalog on the random number field. A listing of the randomly ordered catalog would provide an unlimited source of random samples for future users. In light of the cost and difficulty in selecting a random sample by hand from either a printed catalog or a card catalog, and in light of the many interesting and useful studies that can be made from such samples, it is recommended that librarians with access to automated catalogs consider the possibility of preparing such randomly ordered versions for use by the library community.

References

1. Edward G. Holley and Donald D. Hendricks, *Resources of Texas Libraries,* Texas State Library, Austin 1968.
2. O. Morgenstern, *The Accuracy of Economic Observations,* 2nd. ed., Princeton, 1963.

6 On Economic Growth of Nations and Archival Acquisition Rates

6.1. Introduction

De Solla Price (Refs. 1 and 2) has been one of the most compelling and original advocates of studying the structure of the body of scientific publication as well as its content. His efforts have been handsomely rewarded by a series of striking discoveries of statistical uniformities in the growth rates and distribution of scientific periodical literature, and, by implication, in the distribution of scientific effort and accomplishment.

These results are clearly of practical importance in the allocation and management of resources devoted to scientific research, but they perhaps have an even greater significance in their provision of a wedge opening the study of history to the process of measurement, and, ultimately, of prediction.

It is therefore of more than casual interest to determine whether de Solla Price's uniformities are characteristic of pure science, or whether they typify a more general uniformity in the relationship of human intellectual activities to the channeling influence of civilization's material aspects.

In this paper we describe a uniformity relating the rate at which the Library of Congress acquires books written in the various languages of the world to the economic growth rates of nations. Here the role of pure science is much diminished, but the observed uniformities are somewhat more precise than those described in Reference 2. Indeed, the statistical relationship is so striking that there is a very real temptation to let the tail wag the dog—that is, to attempt to predict the economic state of nations from the much more easily obtained Library of Congress acquisition data, especially for those nations for which reliable economic statistical data are not available. There is no need to dwell on the dangers inherent in such a procedure.

The less tempting but far more reliable use of economic indicators as primitive normative measures of library holdings regarding their distribution in various languages offers, we believe for the first time, an unbiased

115

tool which library management can use to anticipate certain aspects of future demands on the collection, and to plan accordingly.

In Reference 2, de Solla Price observed that national shares of world gross national product (GNP) at a given time are approximately equal to national shares of scientific papers appearing in *Physics Abstracts* or in *Chemical Abstracts* at about the same time. Most of the relevant available statistical data were not collected with such an application in mind; consequently, there are a number of procedural problems concerned with the comparability of statistics obtained from different sources and relating to different years. In general, the uniformity is so evident that, at least in the current state of such studies, the effort of a thorough and documented analysis of sources is not repaid by significant changes in the results.

6.2. The Main Result

Our principal observation is that *the share of Library of Congress non-serial acquisitions written in a given language and bearing a given imprint date is approximately equal to the annual share one decade earlier of world gross national product corresponding to all nations speaking that language.* That there should be a time lag between the GNP year and the related LC acquisitions is quite reasonable, if indeed there is any relation at all. That this period is ten years is incidental and is due to the limited LC statistics available, which are presented in 7.5 year groupings in Reference 3. A more detailed year-by-year study of LC acquisitions, based upon a larger sample than that used in Reference 3 will undoubtedly revise the time lag somewhat. We shall not treat this point further in this chapter.

In their useful paper (Ref. 3), Avram *et al.* describe a random sample of Library of Congress acquisitions in western languages for the period 1950 to 1964. In all, 2224 items are represented in the sample; distributions are given for 1950 to 1957 and for 1957 to 1964. Our Table 23 compares the shares of GNP for 1950 for nations speaking a given language with corresponding shares of LC acquisitions, as given or 1957 to 1964, from Reference 3. Table 24 lists the nations constituting the various linguistic groups for the purposes of this study, with corresponding GNP estimates for 1950, expressed in billions of dollar equivalents in constant 1965 prices. The sources of these figures are described below.

6.3. Omitted Western Languages

Certain languages have been omitted from most of our considerations for various reasons.

Hebrew, ranked fourth in Table 4 of Reference 3, corresponds principally

Table 23   Library of Congress Acquisitions and Gross National Products

Language	1957 to 1964 LC Share	1950 GNP Share	Col. 1 − Col. 2
English	0.562	0.554	0.008
Russian	0.147	0.145	0.002
German	0.081	0.069	0.012
Spanish	0.059	0.047	0.012
French	0.039	0.070	−0.031
Polish	0.030	0.016	0.014
Czech	0.020	0.012	0.008
Italian	0.011	0.031	−0.020
Portuguese	0.011	0.013	−0.002
Dutch	0.011	0.010	0.001
Danish	0.008	0.006	0.002
Swedish	0.007	0.012	−0.005
Bulgarian	0.005	0.004	0.001
Norwegian	0.005	0.004	0.001
Hungarian	0.002	0.005	−0.003

to works published in Israel, but the LC Hebrew acquisition rate of 2.3 percent for 1957 to 1964 is far greater than the Israeli GNP share of 0.08 percent. This discrepancy is explained by the PL 480 authorized use of counterpart funds by the Library of Congress.

Finnish has been omitted because our principal sources of economic statistics (Refs. 4 and 5) do not mention Finland. In any event, less reliable alternative sources indicate that the shares will be approximately 0.005 for LC acquisitions and 0.002 for GNP, confirming the over-all picture.

Latin has been excluded because it is not associated with any nation. If, however, Latin publications are associated with the Roman Catholic Church, and if one construes the Church hierarchy, as opposed to lay Church members, as constituting a fictitious "nation," then our analysis leads to an estimate of "GNP" for the Church for 1950 which appears to be in general agreement with the estimates of our informants. However, we have not attempted to verify the purported agreement.

Ukranian and Serbo-Croatian have been excluded because of the lack of economic data.

6.4. Sources of Economic Statistics

There is no great consistency among the various accessible estimates of foreign gross national products. Thus a few remarks concerning the sources

Table 24 Nations Contributing to Language Group Gross National Product Estimates

Language	GNP*	Nation	GNP*
English	496.1	United States	393.9
		United Kingdom	64.1
		2/3 Canada	16.6
		Australia	11.7
		New Zealand	2.8†
		Ireland	2.0
		U.S. Africa	5.0†
Russian	130	Soviet Union	130.
German	61.5	West Germany‡	41.6
		East Germany	13.0
		Austria	4.2
		1/3 Switzerland	2.7
Spanish	41.9	Spain	8.9
		17 Spanish-speaking	
		Latin American Rep.	33.0
French	62.6	France	46.7
		1/3 Canada	8.3
		1/2 Belgium	4.9
		1/3 Switzerland	2.7
Polish	14.7	Poland	14.7
Czech	10.7	Czechoslovakia	10.7
Italian	28.0	Italy	25.3
		1/3 Switzerland	2.7
Portuguese	11.9	Brazil	10.1
		Portugal	1.8
Dutch	9.3	Netherlands	9.3
Danish	5.6	Denmark	5.6
Swedish	10.8	Sweden	10.8
Bulgarian	3.8	Bulgaria	3.8
Norwegian	3.8	Norway	3.8
Hungarian	4.8	Hungary	4.8
TOTAL	895.5		

*GNP data refer to 1950, and are measured in billions of dollar equivalents in constant 1965 prices.

†Estimated.

‡Includes West Berlin.

of the data assembled in Table 24 are in order. We have relied on Reference 4 prepared by the Agency for International Development in March 1967, for most of our estimates. These are expressed in dollar equivalents of constant 1965 prices and functions thereof, and differ from those presented in the *U.N. Yearbook of National Accounts Statistics* for two reasons: AID uses the aggregate "GNP at Market Prices" whereas the U.N. gives "Gross Domestic Product," and, revisions of national accounts statistics published by several countries since the publication of the relevant *U.N. Yearbook* have been incorporated. Data were obtained from various national publications, from the *U.N. Yearbook,* and from AID and Embassy reports. There appears to be no way to evaluate the relative merit of the extremely varied national statistical data collection processes.

Reference 4 does not provide data for the Soviet Union or the eastern European countries. For the former, we have used the U.S. Department of State estimates prepared by Dr. Herbert Block (Ref. 5). The estimates of GNP for eastern European countries were obtained from the undivided estimate given in Reference 5 for a six-nation combination in the following roundabout way. The 1965 GNP estimates given in Reference 6 for Czechoslovakia, East Germany, Poland, and Romania, and the ratio of the gross national products for 1964 of Bulgaria and Hungary obtained from Table I of Reference 2, were used to establish the relative shares of the total eastern European GNP (defined in Reference 5 as the sum of the GNP's of these six nations) for these nations. With the additional assumption that whatever the growth rate of eastern Europe as a whole, the relative shares of eastern European GNP of these countries did not vary significantly from 1950 to 1965, it is no trouble to estimate the national GNP's for each year in this range from the totals given in Reference 5.

6.5. Library of Congress Acquisitions and GNP

Table 23 shows that the three largest absolute differences between LC acquisition shares and GNP shares are −0.031 (French), −0.020 (Italian), and 0.014 (Polish). In the first two cases, GNP shares are larger than the corresponding LC acquisition shares; in the third, the situation is reversed.

It is relatively easy to underestimate GNP associated with a language group because there are numerous countries, small and large, developed and underdeveloped, that support subpopulations that read and write other than the official language as their native language. The contribution of these pockets, although generally individually quite small, may in the aggregate have a significant effect for certain languages.

Another difficulty in GNP assignment to language groups concerns nations such as Belgium, Canada, and Switzerland with more than one official language. In these cases we have made only the crudest estimates; the linguistic partitions have been accounted for regarding these nations in Table 24 and this is of course reflected in Table 23. The shares of national GNP accruing from the French-speaking subpopulations of Luxembourg, Algeria and other former French-African colonies, etc., have not been estimated. Therefore, the discrepancy between acquisitions and GNP for French is slightly underestimated in Table 23. The same is true of English, but the differences are negligible.

From this point of view, French represents a unique problem in Table 23, the other languages evidencing significant acquisitions-GNP disagreement cannot have had the corresponding GNP underestimated for such reasons. For instance, there are no untapped reservoirs of Italian subpopulations outside of Italy and Switzerland in the senses relevant to this study. But it must also be added that it is not entirely clear that the GNP of individual nations ought to be partitioned according to the linguistic subpopulation shares. Uniform avoidance of partition leads to figures similar to those given in Table 23. We hope to return to this problem in greater depth in another study.

Discrepancies as large as 0.031 in Table 23 are surprisingly small[1] when the general unreliability of GNP estimates and the small size of the Library of Congress sample are considered, but it may still be worthwhile to react as if the acquisitions-GNP share equality were a "law of nature," and so speculate about potential causes of the larger observed discrepancies.

Examination of LC acquisitions in French for 1950 to 1957 in Table 4 of Reference 3 shows that 77 items were acquired during that period, contrasting with the 41 acquired during the 1957 to 1964 base period used in our Table 23. The economic references do not enable one to estimate national GNP shares for 1943 to 1945, a decade prior to the mean of the 1950 to 1957 period, but it is evident that the share due to France, which accounts for the largest part of French GNP, must have been much less than its 1950 share of 0.070, whereas the 1950 to 1957 French share of LC acquisitions (calculated for the languages shown in Table 23) is 0.074. Hence, LC overacquired French during that period, and most likely by a substantial amount. The underacquisition during 1957 to 1964 indicated by Table 24 can then be interpreted as a dynamic feedback response, tending to modify previous departures of acquisition rate from the

---

[1]The absolute values of the corresponding differences for GNP vs. *Physics Abstracts* in Table I of Reference 2 for example, are, in decreasing order: 0.088, 0.043, 0.042, 0.018, etc.; for GNP vs. *Chemical Abstracts* they are 0.051, 0.043, 0.037, 0.025, 0.019, etc.

"natural law" by means of current adjustments. Unfortunately we do not now have sufficient data to check this hypothesis quantitatively, and are, consequently, not convinced that this interpretation is correct; it is, however, highly suggestive and does show the importance of collecting statistical information in this general area of study in a systematic way as part of a continuing program so that dynamical effects can in fact be observed.

Why should Library of Congress acquisition shares approximate national language group GNP shares? Are these two statistics causally related, or is the equality fortuitous—a case of "lying with statistics"? The mechanism used by the Library of Congress to determine which items it will acquire ought to exhibit a structure that would reasonably lead to the observed statistical distribution of acquisitions if there is a causal relation. However, many of the acquisition mechanisms that come most quickly to mind ought not to produce this distribution. In fact, the Library of Congress has about 140 "Recommending Officers" who are associated with various classes of knowledge, and who recommend the acquisition of materials within their field of specialization without formal regard to the origin or language of the item.[2] These recommendations are acted upon within the restrictions imposed by the budget; the latter is not partitioned according to language except insofar as counterpart currencies are available to LC. (At the time of writing, such funds and/or other special funds are available for most of the nations speaking major western languages, so that little bias is anticipated, with the exception of Hebrew.) Each Recommending Officer will be subject to his own linguistic biases; he will more likely have better access to descriptions of materials available in those languages; and he will more likely place a higher value upon a document from a large GNP nation than he would on the same document from a small GNP nation, all other things being equal. These biases of the Recommending Officers are no doubt created in part, and reinforced, by information appearing in the news media, which do react to foreign news in rough proportion to the power of the news-initiating nation, and hence also in rough proportion to their GNP share.

It is not too far-fetched to conceive of the set of Recommending Officers as constituting a statistical ensemble of measuring devices attuned to measure the relative performance of nations within the scope of each Officer's field of specialization. With this interpretation, the equality of GNP shares and acquisition shares emerges as a natural consequence of the LC acquisition selection process.

---

[2]We wish to express our appreciation to Jennifer Magnus, Assistant Chief, Order Division, Library of Congress, for information about the LC order system.

As will be shown later in this paper, the Fondren Library at Rice University (and probably other archival libraries as well) exhibits the same kind of GNP-acquisitions relation. In this case one can argue similarly, noting that the small size of the usual university order staff (which will tend to bias the acquisition structure) is partially offset by the role of the academic staff in acquisitions selection.

Another rather more complicated but also less mentalistic argument suggests itself. It may simply be that the Library of Congress is a random sample of the world's printed matter, and that, therefore, the LC acquisitions-GNP relationship is a natural consequence of the following hypothesis:

> (H) The annual number of books published in a given language is proportional to the combined GNP of the nations using that language, for some related year. Moreover, the constant of proportionality is independent of the nations or languages concerned, as is the time lag separating GNP year from publication year.

The essential part of hypothesis (H) concerns the constancy of the constant of proportionality with respect to language and nation, for otherwise it would be possible to adjust distinct constants to fit the data.

We do not know if (H) is true. Evidence is sparse and less reliable than GNP data even when available, because of varying systems underlying the data-gathering activities of the nations that do provide some type of relevant information. Table 25 displays data from Reference 7 concerning the number of books published in 1964 (in certain cases, 1963) for the United States, Canada, and selected Latin American countries. Corresponding GNP data have been taken from Reference 4, and a "books per billion" ratio of books published to GNP for a given year has been computed.

These ratios, exhibited in the last column of Table 25, fall into three classes:

CLASS I: The United States and Canada, with ratios of 44.3 and 66.7, respectively. These nations have relatively reliable statistics-gathering techniques, and the sample sizes are large. As we shall show below, Canada's bilinguality may account for the difference between these ratios.

CLASS II: Countries with GNP for 1964[3] in the range $10 to $25 billion, including Argentina, Brazil, and Mexico, with ratios of 223, 275, and 253, respectively;

CLASS III: Countries with GNP less than $10 billion. For these, the

---

[3]Measured in constant 1965 dollars.

Table 25   Book Publication Data

Nation	Year	No. of Books	GNP	Books per Billion $ GNP
United States	1964	28,451	643.0	44.
Canada	1964	3,000	45.1	67
Brazil	1963	5,617	20.4	275
Mexico	1964	4,661	18.4	253
Argentina	1964	3,319	14.9	223
Venezuela	1963	743	6.8	109
Peru	1964	946	4.1	231
Chile	1964	1,577	4.0	394
Uruguay	1964	194	1.54	126
Guatemala	1963	90	1.23	73
Dominican Rep.	1963	71	1.01	70
El Salvador	1963	75	0.71	106
Costa Rica	1963	13	0.54	24
Honduras	1964	189	0.47	400

books-per-billion ratio varies from a minimum of 24 (Costa Rica, GNP of $0.536 billion) to 400 (Honduras, GNP $0.47 billion) for the countries listed in Table 25. These countries are unlikely to be equipped to provide reliable statistical information, but moreover, the small absolute size of their publishing industries (the largest in Class III is Peru, 946 titles in 1964, with a ratio of 231, consistent with the pattern of Class II; the next largest is Uruguay, 194 books in 1964, with a ratio of 126) makes the books-per-billion ratio sensitive to relatively small fluctuations of a local nature such as the establishment of a multi-volume national history series by a local university, or the procedure used to classify such items as books or pamphlets, etc. We conclude that Class III nations are too small to be of use in determining the validity of (H) from such data.

The mean of the Class II ratios is 251. Class II includes two language groups; the two Spanish-speaking nations are physically distant and of similar economic size so it is reasonable to assume that there is not a great exchange of published material, although this assumption could presumably be directly checked. Therefore, the three Class II ratios confirm the hypothesis (H) for nations with Class II GNP structure.

The two Class I ratios suggest that the larger national economic units maintain a smaller ratio of publication. If true, this may be related to the per capita growth of GNP, but the significant difference between the ratios for Canada and the United States calls for an explanation. Let us assume that Canada's bilinguality results in excess publication ("excess" with respect to the books-per-billion ratio) measured by the proportion of the

French-speaking population to the whole. If the United States books-per-billion ratio is accepted as typical of Class I nations, then

$$(66.7 - 44.3)/66.7 = 33.6$$

percent of the Canadian population should use French as their principal language; the true proportion, obtained from 1961 Canadian census figures published on page 1203 of Reference 8 showing "(national) origins of the population . . . ," is 30.4 percent. This appears to confirm the idea that the United States and Canada have similar effective books-per-billion ratios.

The presence of distinct ratios for Class I and Class II nations shows that hypothesis (H), in the strict form in which it is stated, is false. However, a weaker form wherein the constant of proportionality is not universal but depends on the general GNP range of the given argument nation, is confirmed by the limited data we have studied. Such a weakened hypothesis still would provide a useful tool for estimating publication growth.

This form of the hypothesis naturally directs attention to the problem of changes of the books-per-billion ratio with time. Figures are available for the United States from 1900 through 1962 for the number of books published in each year (cf. Refs. 9 and 10). These are exhibited, together with United States GNP in current prices, and in 1929 prices (also taken from References 9 and 10) in Figure 19. With the exception of the book-publication depressions due to the two world wars (but not to the economic depression that began in 1929!) GNP and number of books published are roughly in proportion. But more extensive research will be necessary to clarify the consistency and universality of this relationship.

It may be well to note here that the number of books published annually is certainly not proportional to population. Indeed, as one partial confirmation of the hypothesis, we note that long-term library growth rates are consistently exponential in form (see Chapter 5) as is the GNP for this country (neglecting short-term transients induced by depressions, wars, etc.) and that these growth rates are similar: the long-term values for a mature library (such as the Library of Congress) and for the GNP (measured in constant dollars) are both about 3-4 percent per year.

6.6. Language Distribution of Mathematical Journal Titles

For additional evidence concerning the basic acquisitions-GNP relation in settings more general than that provided by the Library of Congress one can examine characteristics of specific types of publications.

De Solla Price studied the serials *Physics Abstracts* and *Chemical Abstracts* in References 1 and 2, in 2 particularly with regard to the

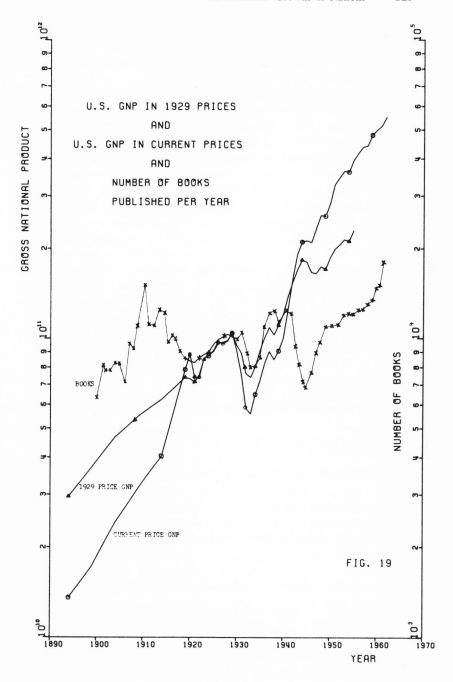

FIG. 19

national origins of papers rather than the language in which they were written. If we sum the contributions of nations speaking the same language given in Table I of Reference 2, the agreement with corresponding language group GNP shares is slightly improved.

Another kind of comparison can be made. One would anticipate that the number of journals in a fixed field published principally in one given language would be proportional to the number of papers produced in that field by the group of nations using that language. We have tested this conjecture for mathematical journals. The serial *Mathematical Reviews* from time to time publishes a list of abbreviations of names of current mathematics journals for bibliographical reference use. Using this data base for 1964, one or more languages has been associated with each journal title according to the following scheme:

1. If the title is in Latin, assign the journal to the language of the publishing nation

2. If the title is in one language different from Latin, assign the journal to the language of the title, regardless of the origin of publication

3. If the title is multilingual, with N languages used, and if none of them is Latin, assign 1/N of the journal to each of the title languages.

As these are the only occurring cases, the above scheme is sufficient to assign journals or aliquot portions thereof to languages in a unique way. Naturally it will often be the case that monolingually titled journals publish substantial portions, perhaps almost all, of their papers in other languages, so that one should not expect very much from so gross an assignment procedure.

With these conventions, there were 842 distributed journal titles listed in the 1964 volume of *Mathematical Reviews*. Of these, 11.5 correspond to non-Western languages:

Chinese	5
Japanese	4
Indian	2
Malaysian	0.5

Table 26 lists the shares of mathematical journals of the languages listed in Table 4 of Reference 3 together with the corresponding LC acquisition shares (for monographs!) for 1950 to 1957 from the same source. The general agreement shown in Table 26 is, we think, remarkable when the grossness of the journal-to-language assignment process is considered. Certainly a direct language count of the papers published in these journals would provide a more reliable statistical indicator of any relations with GNP or LC acquisitions. But the correspondence shown in Table 26 is

Table 26   Language Distribution of Mathematical Journal Titles vs. Library of Congress Acquisition Distribution

| | Math J. Titles | | LC Acq. (1950 to 57) | |
	No.	Share	No.	Share
English	331.83	0.438	500	0.473
Russian	115.	0.152	145	0.137
German	86.5	0.114	136	0.128
Spanish	38.	0.050	67	0.063
French	82.5	0.109	77	0.073
Polish	16.5	0.022	8	0.016
Czech	9.5	0.013	17	0.016
Italian	45.67	0.060	20	0.019
Portuguese	13.	0.017	20	0.019
Dutch	16.	0.021	18	0.017
Danish	5.	0.007	12	0.011
Serbo-Croatian	4.5	0.006	9	0.008
Swedish	13.	0.017	13	0.012
Bulgarian	4.	0.005	6	0.006
Norwegian	9.	0.012	4	0.004
Finnish	7.	0.009	5	0.005
Hungarian	11.	0.015	3	0.003

certainly a confirmation of the general correctness of our principal observations, and a powerful indication that further effort to relate publication and library structure to other structures of a more usual variety will be successful and useful.

Returning for a moment to the data base used to prepare Table 26, we observed that the number of journals published in each country is not proportional to the GNP share of that country. For instance, the United States, Soviet Union, Japan, and Germany (both East and West Germany) are the ranking national publishers of mathematical journals, accounting for 132, 119, 76, and 73, respectively. The shares represented by these numbers bear no relationship to corresponding GNP shares. Indeed, of the 76 journals published in Japan, only 4 have Japanese titles; the remainder are principally English. Similarly, the United Kingdom publishes 60 journals, almost half as many as the United States, but the ratio of United Kingdom to United States 1964 GNP is only 0.15.

6.7.   GNP as a Library Management Tool

The equality of language group GNP shares and LC acquisition shares can be used as a management tool for estimating future allocation of resources for foreign language acquisitions. For instance, a study of the time variation of language group GNP shows that, during the past 15 years at least, growth has been approximately exponential for each major language. If the next 40 years are free of major wars and current economic growth rates are maintained, GNP will be partitioned as shown in Figure 20. If there are significant changes in the component national growth rates, the partition shown should still be generally valid for the next 15 to 20 years, approximately through 1985.

Whereas the English language share of GNP was 55 percent in 1950, it fell to 53 percent in 1955, 49 percent in 1960, and in 1970 it is likely to stand at 46 percent. By 1985 it will have been reduced (using a naive estimating procedure) to 40 percent, and, if conditions remain stable for a further 15 years, the year 2000 will see it at 35 percent. These estimates concern themselves only with the language groups listed in our Table 23 in particular, all oriental languages and the corresponding GNP's have been omitted from the calculations. Consequently, the English language share of world GNP will be further reduced, and, if Japan continues its unusually high growth rate and the other major Asian nations equal the mean growth of the English-speaking nations, the rate of reduction will actually increase. It follows that those libraries which have an acquisition schedule whose language shares approximate the LC language acquisition shares must look forward to a sharply decreasing fraction of English acquisitions, and a corresponding increased demand for librarians—particularly catalogers—with foreign language expertise. The languages in demand will shift to emphasize the Slavic and oriental origins of the acquisitions. For the period 1970 to 1985, about a 12 percent increase in foreign language acquisitions for those languages listed in Table 23 should be anticipated; if our assumptions remain valid through the year 2000, the increase from 1970 to 2000 will be approximately 25 percent.

As noted above, these estimates ignore the rapid growth of portions of Asia. Japanese growth is currently projected at 7.5 percent per annum, whereas most of the rest of the industrialized world looks forward to gains of 4.5 percent (Ref. 5); the absolute magnitude of the shares of China, India, and Indonesia will further contribute to the influx of foreign language holdings and the decrease in the share of the traditional languages.

Many libraries are currently experiencing the growth of a reservoir of uncatalogued acquisitions, in English as well as foreign languages, which exhibits its own annual growth rate. The further severe strains that will be imposed by the increasing proportions of incoming materials in exotic languages may well prove impossible to resolve in the current context of cataloging and processing procedures. In fact, it is not clear that the straightforward computerized and semicomputerized systems that have

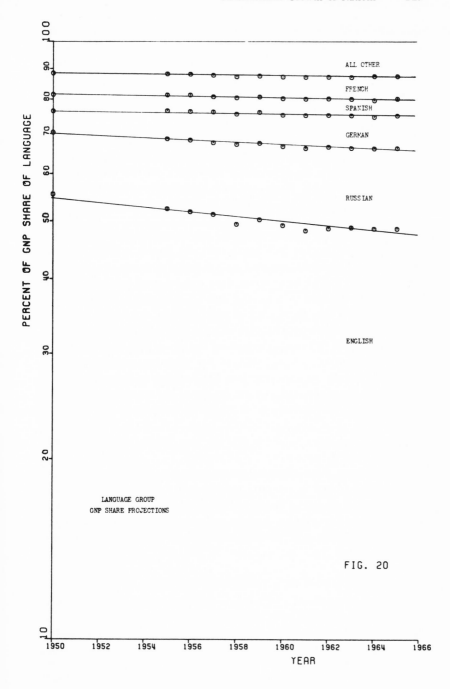

been proposed for various segments of library operations will be any more able to cope with the increasing flood and widening language distribution of acquisitions than current procedures. We believe that the exponential growth rates involved in the various parts of the acquisition process may require a fundamental reconsideration of both the form of storage of information in libraries, and the process flow involved from initial order to final insertion of the holding into the functional collection. Direct automation of current procedures will simply postpone many of the basic growth problems for one or two doubling periods, which, for many university collections, is now less than 15 years.

The fact that acquisitions grow at essentially the same rate as Gross National Product, although much more rapidly than population, implies that it is within the means of the economy to support and maintain library growth. However, since library growth is substantially greater than population growth in this country, it follows that the usual human utilization of libraries (measured by number of items circulated per borrower, for instance) will *decrease* with time. The available data appear to show this trend for the past 40 years. If librarians find it necessary to justify continued library growth on the basis of a circulation per borrower index (rather than on the principle that libraries are the repositories of human knowledge and should therefore grow in proportion to that knowledge, hence with GNP) then circulation will have to be stimulated to maintain growth. Elementary calculations show that human inquiries cannot possibly match acquisitions in growth; thus it follows that libraries will have to gird themselves for responding to machine inquiries if they are determined to maintain circulation rates at or near current levels.

It is quite clear that many interesting problems can be so arranged that machine processing of large amounts of information will provide summary information important to their solution. Hence, future use of machines as information retrieval and summarizing devices operating on the library collection, or on data files which themselves summarize or abstract aspects of the collection, is highly probable. This entails, at the very least, an automated library catalog.

6.8. Comparison of Archival and University Libraries

The Fondren Library of Rice University contains about 275,000 nonserial cataloged volumes. A random sample of 1926 cards drawn from the shelf list led to the distribution by language and year shown in Table 27 for nonserial books.[4] This approximates an acquisition distribution but the

[4]If only copyright year was given, it was used in place of publication year. Some cards showed neither; these were excluded in the construction of Table 27.

Table 27   Fondren Library Language Distribution by Imprint Date

		Number by Language	
	1950 to 56	1957 to 64	1950 to 64
English	172	304	476
German	29	49	78
French	18	24	42
Italian	5	12	17
Spanish	4	8	12
Russian	0	5	5
Portuguese	1	6	7
Polish	1	1	1
Japanese	0	1	1
Icelandic	2	0	2
Dutch	0	1	1
TOTALS	232	411	643

Table 28   Fondren Library Language Distribution for Western Languages by Imprint Date

		Share by Language	
	1950 to 1956	1957 to 1964	1950 to 1964
English	0.742	0.742	0.742
German	0.125	0.120	0.122
French	0.078	0.059	0.065
Italian	0.022	0.029	0.026
Spanish	0.017	0.020	0.019
Russian	0.	0.001	0.001
Portuguese	0.004	0.001	0.001

two are not quite the same thing; we will use it for comparison with the LC data. Table 28 shows the share distribution for Western languages by imprint date for the portion of the Fondren sample with imprints in the interval 1950 to 1964. This distribution is strikingly different from that given in Table 24 for the Library of Congress; the order of languages, ranked by share, is different, and the shares themselves appear to show an overconcentration on English. In each of the three columns of Table 28 more than 95 percent of the Fondren (nonserial) holdings are included in four language groups.

Suppose that we examine the distributions of Library of Congress acquisitions and of gross national products for these four language groups: English, German, French, and Italian. Table 29 exhibits a comparison of the Fondren distribution with the corresponding one for the Library of

Table 29   Library of Congress–Fondren Library Comparison

| | 1957 to 1964 | | | | |
| | LC | | Fondren | | |
	No.	Share	No.	Share	Col. 2 – Col. 4
English	591	0.810	304	0.782	0.028
German	85	0.117	49	0.126	−0.009
French	41	0.056	24	0.062	−0.006
Italian	12	0.016	12	0.031	−0.015
	1950 to 1964				
	LC		Fondren		
	No.	Share	No.	Share	Col. 2 – Col. 4
English	1091	0.746	476	0.776	−0.030
German	221	0.151	78	0.127	0.024
French	118	0.081	42	0.068	0.013
Italian	32	0.022	17	0.028	−0.006

Table 30   Comparison of the Complete Fondren Sample, The Library of Congress Sample, and 1950 Gross National Product Shares

	Complete Fondren[*] 1829 cards	Library of Congress 1950 to 1964	1950 GNP Share
English	0.772	0.746	0.765
German	0.123	0.151	0.095
French	0.083	0.081	0.097
Italian	0.022	0.022	0.043

[*]Includes all nonserial, nonmap book items. Shares are determined from a title count; multivolume works corresponding to one title are counted as one item.

Congress for the periods 1957 to 1964 and 1950 to 1964. There is a rather striking agreement; the largest difference, in absolute value, is 3 percent. Table 30 displays the shares of the *complete* nonserial Fondren sample, the LC acquisition sample (1950 to 1964) and the 1950 share of GNP for the four languages under consideration. Once again agreement is evident without the application of the apparatus of statistical correlation theory. This has the consequence that we can assert that the growth of the Fondren collection has been essentially uniform with regard to the four languages we are now discussing. Consequently, for the Fondren at least, random samples of the entire collection do not differ much from random samples of current acquisitions as far as the major trends are concerned.

This correspondence does, however, overlook the small but rapidly changing phenomena, such as the incipient growth of Russian-language acquisitions, which lie outside of the domain of the four high-ranked language groups.

6.9. Conclusion

It is clear that the Fondren statistics and LC statistics are closely related and it is no less clear that similar statements must hold for most large university libraries. This shows that the relationship between acquisitions and gross national product observed for the Library of Congress is not a phenomenon peculiar to that institution, but rather represents a general characteristic of libraries which are principally devoted to the maintenance of an archival collection.

References

1. D. J. de Solla Price, *Science Since Babylon*, Yale University Press, New Haven, 1962.
2. _____, "Research on Research," *Journeys in Science*, University of New Mexico Press, Albuquerque, (1967) 2-21.
3. H. D. Avram, K. D. Guiles, and G. T. Meade, "Fields of Information on Library of Congress Catalog Cards," *Library Quarterly* 37 (1967) 180-192.
4. "Gross National Product: Growth Rates and Trend Data, by Region and Country," The Agency for International Development, Report RC-W-138, 31 March 1967.
5. H. Block, Table 1. "GNP Series for Selected Areas, 1950-1970," prepared at the U.S. Department of State for the Society for International Development and Association for Comparative Economics, data through 1965; revised for the Soviet Union through January 1967.
6. H. Kahn and A. J. Wiener, *The Year 2000*, The Macmillan Co., New York, 1967.
7. *Statistical Abstract of Latin America*, The University of California at Los Angeles, Los Angeles, 1966.
8. *Canada Yearbook*, 1962.
9. *Historical Statistics of the United States: Colonial Times to 1957*, U.S. Department of Commerce.
10. *Historical Statistics of the United States: Continuation to 1962, and Revisions*, U.S. Department of Commerce.

7 The Use of Machine-Readable Catalog Data in the Production of Bibliographies

7.1. Introduction

The economic aspects of library card catalog conversion to and maintenance in machine-readable form and the utility of such a file as an information base for library management and general research purposes have been discussed in the previous chapters of this report. In this chapter the role of the catalog as a bibliographic tool is considered and various advantages and disadvantages of machine-readable and card catalogs are explored in this context.

We have adopted the following definition, which is convenient for the present purposes:

A *bibliography* is a human-readable ordered list of descriptions of books and/or documents.

The term "human-readable" distinguishes printed materials from non-printed machine-readable materials; for the purposes of this study, whether or not it is necessary to make use of a supplementary machine (such as an optical magnifier) to enable the human to read a human-readable document is immaterial. It must be emphasized that two bibliographies which differ only in the order of arrangement in their entries are different bibliographies according to this definition. We shall be deliberately vague about what constitutes a "description" of a book or document in order to avoid a lengthy discourse on the multifarious ways in which books and documents can be described along with the many ways users can expand their knowledge of a book or document by relating the information provided by one source to that available in another. Nevertheless, we shall assume that a bibliography contains some explicit identification of each book and document (such as the author and title) and some explicit information

135

about its availability (such as the publisher, class number, or location) for each item that it cites.

Our definition is not restricted to those bibliographies that are published for general use. Indeed, many if not most of the lists that would be classified as bibliographies by this definition are of an ephemeral nature and designed for the use of as few as one or two members of the staff or users of a particular library. Examples might be "A list of the books on loan at the XYZ Library on June 15, 1968," and "A list of books on order from South American publishers as of February 29, 1968."

7.2. The Nature of "Standard" Bibliographic Files

To even the sophisticated library user it comes as something of a shock to learn of the large number of files maintained by libraries. According to a recent survey (Ref. 1), the Library of Congress maintains more than 1200; several years ago Stanford University surveyed its file structure and found more than 400, which it has since reduced to approximately 150. Many of these should be classed as correspondence files rather than bibliographic files, but even after this is done the residue of bibliographic files is still substantial. As a gauge of this, consider the following incomplete list of bibliographic files that even libraries of modest size will maintain:

Books requested by library users
Books approved for purchase
Books ordered but not received
Books in transit
Books received
Books awaiting cataloging
Books awaiting shelving
Books on loan
Books lost
Books discarded
Books awaiting repair
Books on indefinite loan
Books requested for interlibrary loan
Books on reserve
Periodicals to be bound
Backlog requests for books on loan.

Clearly file maintenance is an essential feature of library management. The staff must be able to respond to user requests for location information; the current state of commitment of the acquisitions budget must be available; follow-up correspondence with booksellers must be based on accurate information about what has been received; staff expansion requests must be based (in part) on current and reliable estimates of the size and nature of work backlogs, etc.

From one point of view, the essential and unique "product" produced by the library staff is its collection of bibliographic files; they provide the user with an otherwise unavailable means for accessing the body of knowledge amassed by civilization in the course of its history. The bulk of stored information is now generally so vast that the typical user could neither presume the existence of the item he needs, nor hope to locate it without this access capability. A library depends on its bibliographic files just as a skyscraper depends on its elevators.

The cataloging operation introduces a dichotomy in techniques for maintaining the bibliographic files: prior to cataloging, book and document descriptions are incomplete, and, in their early stages, possibly inaccurate; after cataloging, these descriptions are complete and in permanent form for most items, unless massive recataloging efforts are later undertaken. The files of "precataloged" items are highly unstable, subject to continual changes in item descriptions as well as current status indicators, whereas the "postcataloged" files are quite stable and activity on a per unit basis drops sharply. (Statistics show that the annual circulation of large public libraries is approximately three times collection size—approximately equal to collection size for large university libraries. Thus a shelf list circulation file would normally be accessed between one and three times the number of records it contains annually; a "Books requested" or "Books on order" or almost any other precataloged file will service many more inquiries per record per year, in part because the records change rapidly but the number of records in the file varies more slowly.)

The distinction between precataloged files and postcataloged files is reasonable from the users' points of view. Although we shall argue that users have greater needs for access to the precataloged files than librarians generally assume, it is nevertheless true that postcataloged files, containing full bibliographic descriptions, are their principal tool. Therefore, in what follows we will assume that all records pertaining to the actual or prospective holdings of a given library are partitioned into two main files which we will call the *order file* and the *catalog file*. Let us emphasize that by "order file" we mean the totality of information about books not yet cataloged, not just the information pertaining to books actually on order, and that the order and catalog files are each composed of a number of files in the usual sense.

The establishment of these conventions enables us to examine the programs and possibilities of automating the production of bibliographic lists from the order file and the catalog file.

7.3. Automation of the Order File

Considerable insight into the utility of automating the order file can be gained from a study of the progress of the automated system at the University of Newcastle-upon-Tyne Library (Refs. 2 and 3). In the Newcastle system, information is introduced in machine-readable form as a by-product of typing orders to be placed with booksellers. Orders are individually typed and are collected using the computer by means of a straightforward sorting operation so that they are grouped according to bookseller on output.

The Newcastle file is updated with new information on a weekly basis. Various codes are used to indicate difficulties encountered in obtaining individual items. As the date of order is available in the file, information about the time elapsed since placement of an order is always available for query for all books not yet received. Further updating occurs when items are received. Items received that were not ordered (e.g., gifts) are also entered in this file so that it serves as a "recent accessions" file as well as an order file.

Because the Newcastle catalog file is not yet in machine-readable form, there is no direct tie from the order file to the catalog file. This would not inhibit the manual generation of the information necessary to delete entries individually as cataloging of the books received is complete. However, as a cost-reducing feature, received books are automatically deleted from the order file 10 weeks after date of receipt. This raises the possibility that if there is a delay in cataloging, a certain portion of the books will be in limbo: the records will be automatically purged from the order file, but not yet inserted in the catalog file. The main cost of this lapse in control is the cost of obtaining unwanted duplicates through lack of knowledge that the book already exists in the system. However, in the most recent year for which statistics were available, only one unwanted duplicate was actually obtained and this is obviously a small price to pay for elimination of the need to purge the file manually. (Although published reports on this system make no mention of the possibility, a weekly list of purged items would form a useful checklist for the cataloging department.)

Of greater interest to us in this study are the weekly and monthly listings routinely prepared by the system for exploitation of the information on file. Mention has already been made of the use of the file for preparing orders and for listing the accessions. According to Reference 13 the complete set of listings is shown in Table 31. The statistical summary includes counts (and expenditures) by country of origin, average time on order by agent, and various breakdowns of expenditures by fund and country of origin.

Table 31   Standard Reports Generated in the Newcastle Order System

1. Weekly list of new orders (by bookseller)
2. Weekly list of complete file (by author)
3. Weekly list of new accessions (by accession number)
4. Monthly list of new accessions (by fund)
5. Monthly list of bookseller reports (by author)
6. Monthly list of unobtainable items (by author)
7. Monthly list of donors of presented books (by donor)
8. Monthly list of overdue orders (by bookseller)
9. Weekly condensed list of outstanding items (by author)
10. Monthly cumulative financial summary of books received in the current fiscal year (by fund)
11. An eight-part statistical summary

It seems clear that most, if not all, of the information noted would be of great use to most libraries with, perhaps, a different frequency of publication and/or different orderings. It is not too difficult to devise further listings that would be of use, such as the listing of "purged" items received 10 weeks previously for use in checking progress in the cataloging operation. Although some of the above listings would be of use to the library user (e.g., the weekly list of new accessions), the information produced by this system is tailored to the needs of the librarian. User-oriented subject access to the considerable file of recent publications on order and received (but not catalogued) could be provided by making use of the title information, for example.

Even if the temptation to extend the amount of information provided by such a system is set aside, it is still clear that what is available from this computer-oriented system of *bibliographically incomplete* records is quite substantial. When one adds the full bibliographic description to the system and has access to the retrospective file, the possibilities for exploitation are staggering.

It is therefore pertinent to consider, in this bibliographically simple context, just how the authors of the Newcastle system have managed to generate so many obviously useful listings of information. Each record in the file is composed of a number of *fields* of information (some of which may be empty) such as: author, title, bookseller, accession number, fund, date of order, and date of receipt. To generate one of the Newcastle listings, it is only necessary to specify three things: 1) A selection field (or fields) and operation, 2) A sort field (or fields) and operation, and 3) The format of the output list. The selection field(s) determines which records are to be selected from the main file and the sort field(s) determines the order in which these records are to be listed. The selection operation specifies how the selection is to be made, and the sort operation defines the sorting (or "filing") rules to be followed. Format control permits the contraction of record size by deletion, truncation, and abbreviation of fields.

For example, to produce the weekly list of new orders by bookseller, the selection field is the *date of order* field and the selection criterion is that the order date must lie within the current week. The sort field is the *bookseller* field and the order operation is, for instance, normal alphabetic ordering (perhaps with suppression of leading articles). Similarly, the monthly list of new accessions is obtained by selecting the *date of access* field, comparing it with the current date (but now just the *month* portion of the current date) and ordering by *fund name* alphabetically.

Either of these listings could have been produced separately without recourse to the general structure sketched before, or indeed without recourse to the main file itself.[1] As the new orders are produced in a batch and introduced into the system as a single set of records, it would be possible (and might be economically desirable) to write a special program that would generate the weekly list of new orders by bookseller from this information alone. The variety of listings already in use at Newcastle makes it clear that a single programming structure capable of generating *any* of the listings needed is a valuable tool, regardless of whether special programs are added to the system to obtain local economies for particular tasks.

The Newcastle library was, of course, fortunate in its physical and temporal location: a setting where many similar studies were being conducted for other purposes—computer typesetting, information retrieval, studies of archival records—and hence was able to inherit access to experienced computer programmers as well as whole sets of programs that could be adapted for many of their subtasks. Not all public or university libraries will be so fortunate. However, developments in this field to date indicate that there is sufficient general software available (such as the select, sort, and format capabilities necessary for order system reports) so that in the not too distant future librarians can hope to specify the general capabilities they must have to accomplish their set of tasks rather than list individual tasks for which they need specific computer programs. This will both simplify the problem of communicating their needs to the computing world and will improve the probability that their needs will be satisfied.

---

[1]We are informed that the *bookseller* list was in fact produced as a separate listing in the Newcastle system.

As a final remark on the order system file, but one that also generalizes to other portions of library file operations, the Newcastle authors note that: "This is a system that must be justified for its increased efficiency and additional facilities rather than for any savings in staff." (Ref. 3.)

7.4. Determining the Number of Listings

It is clear from what has been said that it is both possible and desirable to list a file in a number of different orderings. It would be helpful to determine from the characteristics of a given file how many orderings might usefully be constructed. In part, this will depend on the size of the file (the larger the file, the more difficult the access; hence the greater the need for different orderings) and in part it will depend on the structure of the individual records: the more fields per record, the more possibilities for new orderings.

Let us assume then that we are investigating a large file and first wish to determine the maximum number of orderings possible. To compute this, it is necessary to distinguish between fields that can be ordered by item and fields that can only be ordered by class. We shall say that a field can be ordered by *item* if there is an almost one-to-one correspondence between the bibliographic items and the contents of the field corresponding to those items. The title field would fit this definition (except for the occasional duplication of titles) if we ignore the existence of multiple copies and include the edition statement with the title. Accession number and author would also be sufficiently close to a one-to-one correspondence to be considered as item fields.

Otherwise, we shall say that a field provides *class* order. Date of publication, place of publication, language, and subject would all be examples of class fields, as there will normally be many items for any particular date of publication, place of publication, etc.

The need for this distinction arises as soon as we recognize that a bibliography in any of its usual realizations (a set of catalog cards or a printed list) is a linear string: each entry (except for the first and last) is directly preceded by another entry and each entry is directly followed by another entry. Hence, to produce a bibliography we must be able to specify the unique ordering that defines it. Specification of the date of publication is not sufficient to define a bibliography: it can only be used to break the entire catalog into subsets wherein the date of publication is the same for all of the items in any subset. Another field must be used to determine the final ordering.

This need is perhaps nowhere more evident than in library shelf lists. The subject field is not naturally an item field, it is a class field: there are not only many titles in the general subject class, *mathematics,* but there are also many titles in the specific subject class, *elementary calculus,* as can be attested to by any mathematics faculty committee concerned with choosing next year's elementary calculus text. However, it is useful to gather books related by subject together on the shelf in a library—for browsing purposes, at least. But it is also necessary to provide a unique location for each book so that the user can readily determine whether a given book is actually on the shelf. This is normally done by constructing a class number based on a fine division by subject, and then within this fine division, obtaining the item order by author (or by a sufficient number of characters in the author's surname).

We now introduce the following notation:

Let N_I denote the number of Item fields in the catalog record, and
Let N_C denote the number of Class fields in the catalog record.

We observe that every ordering of the catalog must have one, and only one, item field in the definition of its ordering. Without such a field, the ordering is not fully defined; once it is fully defined, specification of any other field (item or class) cannot change it. However, we may use anywhere from zero class fields to the total number available (N_C) to define the ordering, as long as these fields take precedence over the item field in the definition of the ordering. With these observations, it is easy to show that the total number of orderings possible is

$$T = N_I \left(1 + N_C + N_C(N_C - 1) + \ldots + N_C! \right)$$

where N! is read as "N factorial" and is numerically equal to the product of all the integers from 1 to N.

The Newcastle order system made use of seven fields to generate the ten reports used in the system. Two of the fields were item fields (author and accession number); the other five were class fields. Substitution of these two values in the formula above shows that they could have generated as many as 652 distinct bibliographies from their system. Although we might argue that with a larger file the Newcastle librarians might have been able to make use of more listings, it seems reasonable to wonder whether *any* library would need 652 distinct listings to manage its order file. Hence we must look for some modification of this formula to take into account the likely use of a file of a given size.

Elsewhere (Ref. 4) we have shown that for certain types of linguistic constructions, the proportion of the possible constructions that actually find use decreases as the complexity of the construction increases and that the rate of decrease is 1/r, where r is approximately equal to 2.5. A trivial example is the following: all English words must contain a vowel. There are five vowels that could stand alone (y can act as a vowel at the end of words, but not at the beginning). Of these, two actually exist as words (a and I), giving a ratio of $5/2 = 2.5$. Introduction of this constant in the preceding formulation gives us a new formula:

$$T = N_I \left(\frac{1}{r} + \frac{N_C}{r^2} + \frac{N_C(N_C - 1)}{r^3} + \ldots + \frac{N_C!}{r^{N_C}} \right)$$

Substitution of $N_I = 2$ and $N_C = 5$ (the Newcastle values) yields $T = 11.47$, which agrees much more favorably with the value of 10 actually found in the Newcastle system.

The order file at Newcastle is a relatively small file when compared to the catalog file at Newcastle or elsewhere, or to the order file of a very large library, such as the Library of Congress. Thus if we accept the notion that as the file grows, there is greater need for access and hence for more listings, it would appear from this formulation that Newcastle is already near the boundary of 11.47 and hence in some difficulty. Actually, Newcastle has four more fields on their order file records (title, publisher, date of publication, and place of publication) that are not presently used in their report system. The title field is an item field and the other three are class fields, yielding a total of three item fields and eight class fields. Substitution of these values in the above formula yields a total of 386 listings, comparable to the number of files maintained for the entire Stanford library, which has in excess of two million monographs alone, prior to their cutback in file maintenance. At present rates of growth, the Newcastle library has ample time to consider adding fields of information to the order system before their order file contains two million or more items.

We do not have good information about how many fields exist in libraries of varying size. Comparing the Newcastle, Stanford, and Library of Congress file figures with their collection sizes, we see that the number of files per thousand items tends to decrease. However, this is not necessarily an indication of how things should be; it may only be a reflection of the fact that maintaining card files is dreadfully expensive when it is necessary to maintain one for each file needed. It may well be that the number of files should grow as fast as the collection, or faster. If we assume that the files should grow as fast as the collection and that the collection grows exponentially (cp. Chapter 2), then it is of interest to inquire how the number of files generated from a catalog record grows as a function of the number of fields of information in the record.

To determine this, we shall assume that the number of item fields is fixed at three (author, title, and accession number), and then compute the number of files as a function of the number of class fields. The results of this calculation are given in Figure 21. The first observation to be made from this graph is that the curve slopes upward, which implies that the growth in number of files produced by a given number of class fields is greater than exponential. (It is a fairly simple mathematical exercise to prove that this is the case.) In other words, even with an exponential growth in the need for files, the length of time a record with a given number of fields will be useful will grow with time. Given the cost of adding fields to the records of large retrospective files, this is a most encouraging development.

Of more immediate interest is the problem of determining the "ideal" number of fields on a record for a library of a given size. According to Figure 21, only eight class fields need to be added to the three item fields to produce the number of files in the Stanford collection, and only nine class fields must be added to match the present LC file collection. However, it should be remembered that these fields must be useful for producing bibliographies. In one version of the MARC II record format, provision is made for approximately 80 fields of variable-length information. A number of these fields will be applicable only to a very small proportion of entries; some are evidently included solely for statistical (as opposed to bibliographic) purposes; and some would be useful only as descriptive material in the context of a particular record, but not for the generation of bibliographies. These questions tend to dominate discussions of what a "complete bibliographic description" should comprise. Our immediate interest in the use of the catalog as a bibliographic tool permits us to avoid this more difficult question and concentrate on those issues relevant for the production of bibliographies. For his purposè, we can make use of the calculations of Figure 21 and then investigate the fields of information that have been used in the production of published bibliographies.

7.5. Potential Candidates for Generation of Bibliographies

Table 31 lists some 50 bibliographies found in the bibliography section of the Stanford University library. This is not a proper random sample but rather a "quickie" list to demonstrate the existence of various types of bibliographies. Using it as a tentative base we can investigate the utility of the various class fields that are (or might be) included in catalog records for the generation of bibliographies.

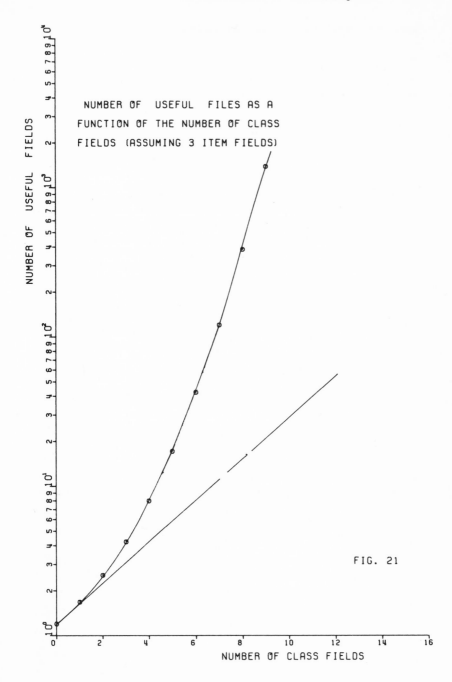

NUMBER OF USEFUL FILES AS A
FUNCTION OF THE NUMBER OF CLASS
FIELDS (ASSUMING 3 ITEM FIELDS)

FIG. 21

Table 32   Some Special-Purpose Bibliographies

1) U.S. Air University Libraries—Special Bibliography
2) Bibliography Documentation Terminology
3) Review of Inter-American Bibliography
4) Current Caribbean Bibliography
5) Bibliographies in Britain
6) Current National Bibliographies
7) Introduction to Bibliography
8) Pan American Union Bibliographic Series
9) The French in North America (a bibliographic guide to French archives, reproductions, and research missions)
10) The Negro in America
11) Bibliography of German Culture in America
12) Dictionary Catalog of the Schomburg Collection of Negro Literature and History (NY Pub Lib)
13) A Layman's Guide to Negro History
14) A Bibliography of the Prairie Provinces to 1953 (published 1956)
15) A Classified Bibliography of the Periodical Literature of the Trans-Mississippi West 1811-1957 (published 1961)
16) Thomas D. Clark Travels in the Old South, 1527-1783 (Vol. 1)
                                              1750-1825 (Vol. 2)
                                              1825-1860 (Vol. 3)
17) Thomas D. Clark Travels in the New South, 1865-1900 (Vol. 1)
                                              1900-1955 (Vol. 2)
18) Life and Literature of the South
19) Bibliography of California Fiction, Poetry, Drama
20) Criticism of California Literature
21) Bibliographies of California Authors and Indexes of California Literature
22) Books and Authors of San Diego
23) The Charlemagne Tower Collection of Colonial Laws
24) Index to Writings on American History
25) Civil War Books—A Critical Bibliography
26) Catalogue of the Military Library
27) Bibliography of National Parks and Monuments West of the Mississippi River

We shall assume the existence of the Author, Title, and Class number fields for specification of item fields. From the arguments of the preceding section, we know that large libraries will need to make use of eight or nine class fields in order to properly exploit the information in their catalog.

The Subject Field

It seems almost unnecessary to dwell on the utility of subject designation for the purposes of generating bibliographies. Scanning through Table

28) Catalog of the Yale Collection of Western America
29) Bibliography of Pennsylvania History
30) The British National Bibliography, 1964
                                  1965
                                  1966
31) American Independence (published 1965)
32) Subject Guide to U.S. Publications
33) The Cambridge Bibliography of English Literature
34) Bibliography of Studies in Victorian Literature
35) A Guide to Irish Bibliographical Material
36) Archaeological Bibliography for Great Britain & Ireland
37) Texts and Calendars (an analytical guide)
38) Bibliography on Writings on the English Language (from Beginning of Printing to End of 1922) (published 1927—author/Kennedy)
39) Annual Bibliography of English Language & Literature
40) Bibliography of Italian Linguistics
41) Elizabethan Translations from the Italian
42) Italian Translations in America
43) Russian & East European Publications in U.S. Libraries
44) Doctoral Research on Russia & the Soviet Union
45) The Kilgour Collection of Russian Literature
46) Monthly Index of Russian Accessions
47) The Pakistan National Bibliography
48) South Asia—an introductory bibliography
49) Indian National Bibliography
50) Early Indian Imprints
51) Guide to Japanese Reference Books
52) Korean Studies Guide
53) Japan—Bibliography of the Humanistic Studies and Social Relations
54) International Bibliography of Historical Sciences
55) Avery Index to Architectural Periodicals (Columbia University—Vols. 1-12)
56) United Nations Documents Index
57) The Literatures of the World in English Translation (Vol. 11—The Slavic Literatures)

32 we see the terms *literature, history, linguistics, architecture, archaeology, poetry, drama,* etc., occurring repeatedly. Indeed, almost any library that maintains a catalog will have a subject-ordered listing (or class-number-ordered listing) that is, in the sense we are using the term here, a subject bibliography. The primary difference between the usual subject catalog in a library and a subject-oriented bibliography is in the fine ordering. The subject-ordering of a library catalog may average as few as two titles per subject (with the item-ordering being established by author or

title within these very small classes). A subject-oriented bibliography will normally use broader subject definitions with many titles per subject. The Widener Shelf List publications (Volumes 1 through 15) have from 1170 titles (*Crusades*) to 83,867 titles (*American History*), each subject class being ordered by classified, alphabetical, and chronological listing. The growth in interest in interdisciplinary studies suggests that capability to produce author- or title-ordered lists of two or more subject headings may prove popular in the future.

Insofar as this capability is concerned, it makes little difference whether the library is using a decimal classification system, the Library of Congress class number, subject words, or some combination of these. It is only essential to be able to identify broad subject headings. The more subject information available, the more flexibility available for the production of such bibliographic listings. However, broad subject definition is all that is required.

Place of Publication

Geography plays an important role in the construction of bibliographies, but one that is difficult to pin down. Geography is in part enumerated in the subject information. In the *Outline of the Library of Congress Classification* we find:

DD   History and Topography (Germany)

JN   Constitutional History and Administration (Europe)

LF   Education (Europe)

PT1-PT3971   Literature (Germany)

all of which could be used as source information to derive a bibliography about Germany. (The refinement of subject classes would surface even more of this sort of information.) Nonetheless, if we were interested in studying the publications of a given country, or area, we would need to make use of the *place of publication* field to ensure coverage of those subject areas that are not normally partitioned by geographic area.

In using place of publication, as in other of the class fields, some items will be missed and other "false drops" will occur due to the fact that authors of one country will publish in another. However, human post-editing of the machine output is possible and would generally be much less expensive (and much more thorough) than human preparation of the original list.

Referring to Table 32, we see that there are a number of entries involving geography:

English Literature
Irish Bibliographic Material
Italian Linguistics
Russian and East European Publications
Early Indian Imprints

and so forth.

The Time Field

Time also plays an important role in the bibliographies of Table 32. We note:

Victorian Literature
Writings on the English Language (beginning of printing to end of 1922)
Early Indian Imprints
Current Caribbean Bibliography

and so forth.

As with place of publication, date of publication is not an infallible guide to the time of preparation of the material. Re-publication of the material, late publication of collected papers, lack of dates on some material, etc., can all cause inadequate dating in the bibliographic record. Nonetheless, time of publication is a valuable access point for any collection. Addition of human editing and use of other key information (such as key words in the titles) can produce sophisticated time-ordered bibliographies. (Subject information also occasionally includes time information:

E351-364   War of 1812
PT6000-6471   Flemish since 1830

and so forth.)

The Language Field

Language information shows up in a variety of ways in the titles in Table 32:

English Literature
Translations from the Italian
Literature of the World in English Translation

and so forth.

Catalog entries do not normally include this information, presumably on the grounds that the reader can determine this for himself from the language used in the title. However, language is used as a tag in the MARC format and is recommended by most workers in the field as an explicit tag to avoid the need for a complex linguistic algorithm to infer the language from the words in the title and other information in the record.

The Bibliography Field

Standard cataloging practice requires that bibliographic notes be added to the entry where appropriate. In Figure 22 we show an analysis of the bibliographic indications given in the cards of the Fondren Sample (see Chapter 5 of this Report). Where no information was indicated, we have counted the item as having zero pages of bibliography. Where the entry is vague about the amount of material ("bibliographic references given in notes") we have assumed one page of such material. Otherwise we have indicated the actual page counts.

Making the arbitrary assumption that five pages is sufficient to provide a significant amount of bibliographic material, we see (Table 33 and Figure 22) that approximately 9 percent of the monographs in the Fondren sample contain significant bibliographies (11 percent if Literature [Class P] is not counted) and that this material far outweighs the number of

Table 33 Number of Items with Five or More Pages of Bibliography in the Fondren Random Sample by LC Class

LC Class	Number of Items	Number of Items with Five or More Pages of Bibliography	Percent of Items with Five or More Pages of Bibliography
A	13	—	—
B	186	18	9.68
C	17	—	—
D	188	19	10.11
E	73	14	19.18
F	53	5	9.43
G	43	—	—
H	211	26	12.32
J	46	5	10.87
K	9	—	—
L	68	6	8.82
M	30	4	13.33
N	75	7	9.33
P	574	33	5.75
Q	206	25	12.14
R	21	2	9.52
S	14	—	—
T	72	1	1.39
U	18	—	—
V	9	—	—
Z	53	22	41.51
Total	1981	187	9.44

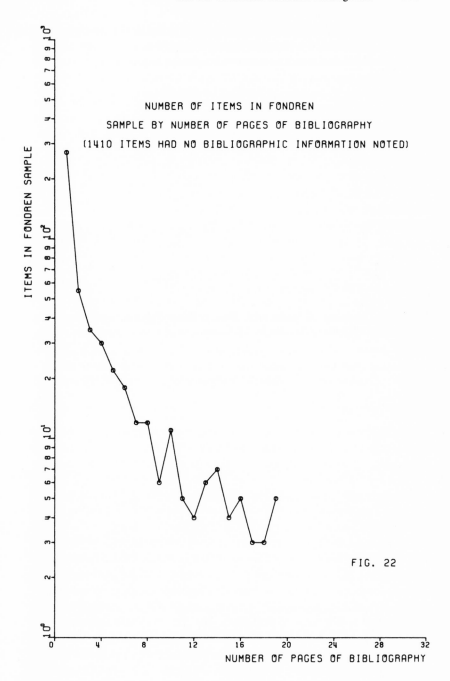

NUMBER OF ITEMS IN FONDREN
SAMPLE BY NUMBER OF PAGES OF BIBLIOGRAPHY
(1410 ITEMS HAD NO BIBLIOGRAPHIC INFORMATION NOTED)

FIG. 22

publications that are explicitly indicated as being bibliographies in the Fondren collection. Nine percent of the collection is much too much to ignore, and yet the yield rate per item searched is clearly too low to permit efficient use of this material if it is not displayed separately. Some libraries do maintain such files and it seems clear that this tag should be used for generating bibliographies.

The Location of Holdings Field

By implication, the inclusion of a record in the catalog of a simple library specifies that the corresponding item is held in that library. The circulation file provides the dynamic mechanism to determine the specific location of the book in the user-library complex. The order file provides the dynamic specification of its location prior to cataloging.

Union catalogs of holdings of particular subject matter with designation of the holding library for each item serve a useful purpose. County library systems using mechanized catalogs can, and do, provide union listings of the entire system because of the particularly simple arrangements for inter-library loans in a county system. Where the holdings have a large degree of overlap this greatly simplifies the task of compiling and printing the catalog. Where the overlap is small, and particularly where the overlap is dictated primarily by subject matter, there may be much to be said for preparing individual catalogs for each library or subcollection in the systems for the users of that library or subcollection.

The Title Field

The title field is basically an item field. It will normally be included in the record for item purposes and is available for use as a class field. Exploitation of the information in the title is a relatively new and sometimes controversial area in library applications. However, the use of permuted title indices to library holdings is growing. Various fields of science, engineering, and mathematics seem to be most suitable at present for exploitation of this type.

In addition, the capability to access every document with certain words in its title in a collection would at least be of use to a trained bibliographer in dropping out items that might otherwise be lost. Extensive use of title-word information implies considerable sophistication in computational linguistics and hence implies the existence of a good programming language that enables one to implement the use of such techniques within reasonable cost and time constraints.

The above enumeration provides us with three item fields and seven class fields, enough according to the graph of Figure 21 to usefully generate approximately 120 catalog files. Not all of these would be complete listings of the file: presumably a listing of the items in the collection that do *not* contain bibliographies would be of little interest; title-word access to some subsets of the collection will be useful where it would not for other subsets.

As noted above, it is not clear how many listings are required to provide proper access to a collection of a given size. Presumably, one or two more fields of information will be necessary for proper exploitation of very large collections. Other information is normally provided in a "complete bibliographic description" and the extensions of that information now under consideration in Project MARC lead us to believe that even with the exponential growth of libraries, standard bibliographic practice will suffice for all libraries except those possessing in excess of several million items for many years to come.

7.6. Other Considerations

The publication of special subject bibliographies can serve a number of purposes. In a large library that is faced with the problem of reprinting its catalog, there is a serious question about the frequency with which the entire catalog can be printed: machine time, composition cost, and the printing cost itself are all substantial factors. Commitment to printing the entire catalog involves commitment to the state-of-the-art printing industry at the then current time and involves a massive effort on the part of the library staff to be sure that the most recent information is available by the deadline for submission to the printer. Furthermore, for a large catalog involving many volumes one can expect a rather long delay from the time the material is submitted to the printer until it is all available and ready for distribution. On the other hand, there is no particular reason why the individual subject volumes cannot be reprinted on, say, a staggered monthly basis, running through the entire list and then starting over again from the beginning. This would reduce the peak load requirements considerably, would permit the library to modify its use of printing equipment to take advantage of recent developments as soon as these developments were available, and would hence do away with the risk of committing a large investment to equipment that might become obsolete during the actual printing process itself. It may well be that continued reprinting of the subject catalog volume by volume, with various orderings within each of these volumes, can do away with the need for printing (or at least with the need for graphic arts quality printing) of the author and title list. This is not to imply that no one of the library staff or users will need access to such information, but rather that most users who wish to make use of author access will be able to specify the general subject heading in which this author or the title is likely to appear and, hence, can obtain the information he needs from the latest printed catalog for that particular subject. Presumably some users will occasionally be troubled by the necessity of looking in two places to find something, but this is the problem of any access system. Under these circumstances, the library could make use of the cheapest possible printed output (probably electronic photocomposition of low graphic arts quality at a very high throughput speed) for its complete author/title list and never have to face the cost of producing a multiple copy graphic arts quality author list or title list.

For these purposes it is not necessary to actually partition the entire catalog into disjoint sets of information. That is, when a particular volume is published it may have some records in common with preceding volumes of the set. One could publish mathematics, for instance, by itself, in conjunction with physics, or in conjunction with physics and engineering, and go through a variety of permutations of this sort so that in one sense any given catalog publication is never really reproduced.

For many purposes an out-of-date catalog is still more than adequate. Hence, by scheduling a set of catalog productions, one can ensure that the most rapidly changing materials are reprinted more frequently than the slowly changing materials and that the mix of the information is continually changing so that the user has access to a wide variety of access points to the holdings of the library. As was remarked above, such a procedure removes the need for the librarian to commit himself to a single plan that must be implemented at once at high cost and instead gives him the flexibility to change with the times.

In open-stack libraries it might be very desirable to have single volumes available at the appropriate places in the stack itself so that the user who is doing a bit of browsing can access the catalog material in the immediate vicinity of the books for which he is searching rather than have to return to a main catalog some distance removed from his location in the stack.

In considering this approach to the publication of the subject catalog it is well to note that in those areas where the user can restrict the demands of his search to a particular subject area and thereby restrict the size of the catalog he must interrogate, he is clearly going to have a much shorter scan time for successful access than otherwise. It is not uncommon for a user to look for a book in mathematics for which he is not sure of the spelling of the author's name or the exact wording of the title. Under these circumstances, if all the potential authors with similarly spelled names could readily be scanned, perhaps on half a page, the user would be able to locate the desired document rather rapidly. On the other hand, if the author name is common and the user has to scan the entire appropriate section of the complete author list, he may have to scan the equivalent of several pages of telephone directory typographic density, and at this point he may decide that the search is not worth it.

7.7. Public Sale of Catalog Information

One point of some importance that should be made in this context is that there is a market of unknown proportions awaiting the sale of library catalogs. Very large and expensive files, of course, have limited distribution. The catalog of the British Museum, the National Union List, and so forth, have cost measured in terms of thousands of dollars, and distribution is primarily limited to very large libraries and other repositories in business and industry. It would be the rare individual user, indeed, who would wish to pay $5,000 or $10,000 to have continuing access to the printed catalog of such a large collection. However, as is pointed out in Chapter 3, it is possible with a machine-readable data base and with modern photocomposition techniques to greatly reduce the cost of catalog information on most any size level. The catalog of the British Museum could be reduced in volume at least by a factor of 5, and perhaps by a factor of 10. To what extent this would extend its saleability to nonlibrary customers is questionable. Further, for documents of this sort one can anticipate that librarians will be the main users and will spend a fair amount of time using at least a set of catalogs if not using a single printed catalog of this sort (we note for instance that in the Widener shelf list volume on bibliography [Ref. 5], that library has acquired over the last dozen years some 150 new library catalogs). Under these circumstances it is not surprising that librarians tend to favor catalogs printed with fairly large type, say 8-point type or larger.

For the occasional user, however, it is quite clear that one could use much finer type, perhaps 5-1/2-point or 6-point, and thereby reduce the cost of producing catalogs and other bibliographies quite substantially. This factor will show up most clearly in relatively small bibliographies or small segments of large catalogs. The first 20 volumes of the Widener shelf list, for instance, are being sold commercially and in its present form, individual volumes sell for $25 or more. The material in these first 20 volumes is all photo-offset reproduction of line printer output, and this, of course, is not the most economical way to produce such material. In a private communication from Mr. DeGenero of the Widener Library we learned that plans have been made to produce at least a few of the future volumes of the shelf list using photocomposition methods to reduce the cost in the hope that these volumes will thus be made available to a wider audience and in particular to an audience of individual users in addition to the usual audience of libraries.

To be sure, not every library has the wealth of material that the Widener Library has accumulated over the years, but then not all requirements for information require this depth. There are at least two major reasons for publishing a subsection of a catalog for widespread use. One is the depth or uniqueness of the material involved in the collection, and the other is the availability of the material to a particular set of users. For a scholar working in a particular field it would obviously be useful to have volumes from large libraries such as the Widener Library to enable him to do in-depth studies in his field of interest. Furthermore, through his local university library he can obtain access to some of these documents because they will also be found in his university library or because he can make use of interlibrary loan service.

At the other extreme the user of the small county library system is primarily interested in determining the availability of materials in his own library system. Thus, in one of the first county library automation projects, the Baltimore County Libraries made available their printed catalogs not only to each of the branches of the system but also to all the schools in the county. Distribution of catalogs is economically possible if printed catalogs are used, and not possible when cards are used; this is frequently put forth as one of the main reasons for making use of printed catalogs in a library system. Clearly, because of the relationship that exists between the county library system and the county school system there are many educational advantages to being able to provide the children of the school system with in-school access to records of library materials.

In between these two extremes there are all degrees and gradations of situations. However, the nature of the collection and its location will still be important factors in the decision of a particular library to make larger print runs of its main catalogs and to develop special subcatalogs of interest to its users. Thus far, with the exception of the production of the Widener shelf list and county and school cooperation such as is illustrated by the Baltimore County Library catalog efforts, librarians have been somewhat slow to assume the responsibility for publication of materials for users as opposed to publication of materials for other libraries. If full advantage is to be taken of automation of the catalog operation, librarians will have to look much more closely at the possibility of publishing materials from their machine-readable catalogs. Potentially, if there were sufficient sales, a particular library might actually offset a substantial portion of its cataloging operation costs through the sale of printed catalogs. In order to explore these possibilities, cautious plans should be prepared to issue various special subcatalogs on a trial basis with the anticipation of breaking even on their cost through public sales.

7.8. Conclusions

The mechanization of large library files provides the library with the opportunity of extending the use of those files through different orderings and orderings of subsets of the information far beyond that which can be maintained in a manually operated file system. We have constructed a model, based on known characteristics of language, that permits us to estimate the number of useful files that can be generated from records of a given structure. To the extent that this model is realistic, it permits us to examine standard cataloging practice and to see that there is sufficient information available in standard cataloging to enable us to produce a number of useful files. The more serious question as to how many files are needed for a collection of a given size will require more study. However, we have studiously ignored the possibility of direct computer access ("on-line access") to the catalog file. As costs of computation come down this will become more and more of a reality, and although we do not expect to see the demise of the printed list, we do expect that on-line access will play an increasingly important role in the exploitation of catalog information.

References

1. United Aircraft Corporate Systems Center, *Survey and Analysis of Bibliographic Apparatus*, Appendix A, "File Census," 1967.
2. Cox, Dews, and Dolby, *The Computer and the Library*, University of Newcastle-upon-Tyne Library, 1966; Archon Press, Hamden, Connecticut, 1967.
3. Cox and Grose, *Organization and Handling of Bibliographic Records by Computer*, Oriel Press, 1967.
4. Dolby and Resnikoff, "On the Structure of Written English Words," *Language*, 40 (1964) 167-196.
5. *Widener Library Shelflist No. 7, Bibliography and Bibliography Periodicals*, 1966, Harvard University Library.

Index

Instructions for Use of the Index

The index is the result of applying an algorithm to the text of the book; a minimal amount of (probably mechanizable) subjective human post-editing in the final two steps produced the amalgamated and reordered form that is printed below.

All word sequences that are not printed in italics appear in the given form in the text of the book, apart from possible differences of capitalization. Terms that do not explicitly appear in the text do not appear as index terms with the exception of the collective Computer Languages, and the alternative World War I for the naturally occurring entry "First World War."

Those readers who are experts in information retrieval and automatic indexing may be interested to know that this is a 4 percent index.